DEAD
FRENCH
POETS
Speak Plain English

Dead
French Poets
Speak Plain English

An Anthology of Poems

Translated by

Kendall Lappin

Kendall Lappin
De Pauw 1938

PARADISE, CA

ASYLUM ARTS

1997

Library of Congress Catalog Number : 97-70311

Book and cover design by Greg Boyd

A Pont Neuf Book

Asylum Arts
5847 Sawmill Road
Paradise, CA 95969

CONTENTS

Dead French Poets

Speak Plain English

FOREWORD

Lyric poetry, that magical fusion of thought, emotion and musicality, is extremely difficult—some say quite impossible—to translate satisfactorily into another language. Consequently, the publication of any book such as this one is almost certain to occasion skepticism and low expectations. Knowledgeable bilingual readers, sensitive to the nuances of both languages, will of course constitute a particularly tough audience; such persons will be well aware that "traduttore, traditore" (every translator's a traitor), and that "translations are like women: if faithful, they're not beautiful, and if beautiful, they're not faithful."

Be all this as it may, dear Reader, you are hereby cordially invited to consider and appraise the following English versions of some classic French poems of widely-varying vintage. Since my selection has been limited to poems perceived as susceptible to scrupulous translation, some of your personal favorites may be missing.

K. L.

TRANSLATOR'S PREFACE

The intrinsic difficulty of accurate translation is greatest when the material being translated is lyric poetry. The translator, in addition to rendering the true and complete *sense* of a foreign-language poem, needs also to make his rendition "sound like poetry." To this end, he must avoid all stylistic awkwardness and obscurity—those pesky defects which so often make an English version "sound like a translation."

Since classic foreign-language poems almost always feature patterned rhyme, translators tend to assume that their own English versions must also rhyme, in precisely the same places. I believe this assumption is a fatal error. The constant pressure of "forced rhyme" makes it virtually impossible to keep an English version both semantically accurate and pleasingly euphonious.

So, rather than "throw in the towel" by resorting to "poetic re-creation," I have resolved just to disregard the rhyme scheme of French poems. After all, *poetic quality* does not reside exclusively in patterned rhyme. Poetic musicality abounds in "blank verse," "free verse" and "prose poems." It derives from such elements as rhythm and flow, *incidental rhyme* and near-rhyme, consonance and assonance, alliteration, and careful choice among synonyms.

Rhythm and flow, in particular, can be systematically emulated via *syllable-counting*. French prosody always requires a specific number of syllables per line (including "mute e" syllables), and a resourceful translator into English can often manage to match the French, line for line, in *syllabic length*. Whenever such matching is accomplished, an element of rhythmic similarity between original and version is achieved.

A wise person once declared that "Any translation of a foreign-language poem must stand on its own merits as a poem in English." Amen. So I strive to render the *music* of each poem, as well as its message.

K. L.

*   *   *

Le temps a laissié son manteau
De vent, de froidure et de pluye,
Et s'est vestu de brouderie,
De soleil luyant, cler et beau.

Il n'y a beste, ne oyseau,
Qu'en son jargon ne chant ou crie:
Le temps a laissié son manteau
De vent, de froidure et de pluye.

Riviere, fontaine et ruisseau
Portent, en livrée jolie,
Gouttes d'argent d'orfaverie,
Chascun s'abille de nouveau.
Le temps a laissié son manteau.

Fair Weather

The weather's put away its cloak
Of wintry wind and freezing rain,
And decked itself in finery,
In beaming sunshine, clear and fair.

No bird nor beast but sings or cries
In its own jargon this refrain:
"The weather's put away its cloak
Of wintry wind and freezing rain."

The river, spring and rivulet
All wear, as pretty livery,
Bright silver drops of jewelry;
Each one is donning new array.
The weather's put its cloak away.

* * *

Les en voulez vous garder,
Ces rivières, de courir,
Et grues prendre et tenir
Quant haut les veez voler?

A telles choses muser
Voit on fols souvent servir:
Les en voulez vous garder,
Ces rivières, de courir?

Laissez le temps tel passer
Que Fortune veut souffrir,
Et les choses avenir
Que l'on ne set destourber,
Les en voulez vous garder?

Would You?

Would you keep from flowing free
Every river, every stream,
Catch and hold high-flying cranes
When you see them on the wing?

Often on such things as these
Fools or madmen tend to muse;
Would you keep from flowing free
Every river, every stream?

Suffer Time to run its course
Just as Fortune will allow
And let be what is to be;
How to change it, one can't know.
Would you stay the river's flow?

* * *

Frères humains, qui après nous vivez,
N'ayez les cuers contre nous endurcis,
Car, se pitié de nous povres avez,
Dieu en aura plus tost de vous mercis.
Vous nous voiez cy atachez cinq sis,
Quant de la chair, que trop avons nourrie,
Elle est pieça devorée et pourrie,
Et nous, les os, devenons cendre et pouldre.
De nostre mal personne ne s'en rie,
Mais priez Dieu que tous nous vueille absouldre!

Se vous clamons frères, pas n'en devez
Avoir desdaing, quoy que fusmes occis
Par justice. Toutesfois, vous sçavez
Que tous hommes n'ont pas bons sens assis;
Excusez nous puis que sommes transsis,
Envers le filz de la Vierge Marie,
Que sa grace ne soit pour nos tarie,
Nous preservant de l'infernale fouldre.
Nous sommes mors, ame no nous harie;
Mais priez Dieu que tous nous vueille absouldre!

La pluye nous a debuez et lavez,
Et le soleil dessechié et noircis;
Pies, corbeaulx, nous ont les yeux cavez,
Et arrachié la barbe et les sourcis.
Jamais nul temps nous ne sommes rassis;
Puis ça, puis là, comme le vent varie,
A son plaisir sans cesser nous charie,

Ballad of the Hanged

O human brothers, living after us,
Let not your hearts against us harden, for
If you have pity on poor souls like us,
God will more likely mercy show to you.
You see us, five or six, still hanging here,
Our flesh, for which we always cared too much,
All rotted, torn to pieces and devoured,
And us, the bones, becoming ash and dust.
Let none with scornful laughter mock our plight,
But pray to God to please absolve us all!

We call you brothers, but for this you must
Not scorn us, though by justice we were slain,
For after all, you know that men are men
And haven't always common sense enough.
Excuse our fault in having greatly sinned
Against the Virgin Mary's blessed Son,
So that His grace be not withheld from us,
And save us from the thunderbolts of Hell.
We're dead, stone dead, so harry not our souls,
But pray to God to please absolve us all!

The rain has washed the mud from off our backs,
The sun has dried us out and turned us black;
The crows and daws have feasted on our eyes
And plucked our beards and eyebrows for their nests.
Not for one moment have we sat to rest;
The wind, now hither, thither as it blows,
Keeps swinging us at will without surcease;

Plus becquetez d'oiseaux que dez à coudre.
Ne soiez donc de nostre confrairie,
Mais priez Dieu que tous nous vueille absouldre!

Prince Jhesus, qui sur tous a maistrie,
Garde qu'Enfer n'ait de nous seigneurie:
A luy n'ayons que faire ne que souldre.
Hommes, icy n'a point de mocquerie,
Mais priez Dieu que tous nous vueille absouldre.

We're more than thimble-marked by pecking birds.
So be not of our brotherhood yourselves,
But pray to God to please absolve us all!

Prince Jesus, Lord and Master over all,
Let Hell not have dominion over us,
Nor us therewith have anything to do.
From you, O men, no mocking laughter here,
But pray to God to please absolve us all!

Joachim DuBellay

* * *

Si nostre vie est moins qu'une journée
En l'éternel, si l'an qui fait le tour
Chasse noz jours sans espoir de retour,
Si périssable est toute chose née,

Que songes-tu, mon ame emprisonnée?
Pourquoy te plaist l'obscure de nostre jour,
Si, pour voler en un plus cler sejour,
Tu as au dos l'aele bien empennée?

Là, est le bien que tout esprit desire,
Là, le repos où tout le monde aspire,
Là, est l'amour, là, le plaisir encore.

Là, ô mon ame, au plus hault ciel guidée,
Tu y pouras recongnoistre l'Idée
De la beauté qu'en ce monde j'adore.

Joachim DuBellay

The Ideal

Though this our life is less than one brief day
In time eternal, though the circling year
Bears off our days without hope of return,
Though every creature born must perish, why,

My captive soul, shouldst thou reflecting pine?
What charm for thee can hold our darkness here
When thou, to fly off to a brighter clime,
Hast on thy back such strong, well-feathered wings?

There lies the good that's every mind's desire,
There the repose to which we all aspire,
There love awaits, there carnal pleasure too.

There, O my soul, to highest Heaven led,
Thou mayest know again that Form Ideal
Of beauty whom in this world I adore.

Joachim DuBellay

* * *

Heureux qui, comme Ulysse, a fait un beau voyage,
Ou comme cestui-là qui conquit la toison,
Et puis est retourné, plein d'usage et raison,
Vivre entre ses parents le reste de son aage!

Quand revoiray-je, helas, de mon petit village
Fumer la cheminée: et en quelle saison
Revoiray-je le clos de ma pauvre maison,
Qui m'est une province, et beaucoup d'avantage?

Plus me plaist le sejour qu'ont basty mes ayeux,
Que des palais Romains le front audacieux:
Plus que le marbre dur me plaist l'ardoise fine,

Plus mon Loyre Gaulois, que le Tybre Latin,
Plus mon petit Lyré, que le mont Palatin,
Et plus que l'air marin la douceur Angevine.

Joachim DuBellay

Nostalgia

Fortunate he who, like Ulysses, travels far,
Or like that what's-his-name who won the Golden Fleece,
Then goes back home, in wisdom and experience rich,
To live among his kin those years still left to him!

Alas! When shall I see again the chimney-smoke
Of my own little village? At what time of year
Shall I behold once more my humble house and close,
Which is to me a province, and a great deal more?

I like far better the abode my forebears built
Than any Roman palace with its bold façade;
I like a fine, smooth slate far more than marble hard,

Lyré's My Gallic Loire far more than Latin Tiber's stream,
My little ▓▓ hill more than the Palatine,
And more than salt sea air, sweet Anjou's gentle clime.

Joachim DuBellay

* * *

Tu ne me vois jamais (Pierre) que tu ne die
Que j'estudie trop, que je face l'amour,
Et que d'avoir tousjours ces livres à l'entour
Rend les yeux esblouis et la teste eslourdie.

Mais tu ne l'entens pas! car ceste maladie
Ne me vient du trop lire ou du trop long séjour,
Ains de voir le bureau, qui se tient chascun jour:
C'est, Pierre mon amy, le livre ou j'estudie.

Ne m'en parle donc plus, autant que tu as cher
De me donner plaisir et de ne me fascher:
Mais bien en ce pendant que d'une main habile

Tu me laves la barbe et me tonds les cheveulx,
Pour me desennuyer, conte moy, si tu veulx
Des nouvelles du Pape et du bruit de la ville.

Sonnet for My Barber

You never see me, Pierre, without reproaching me
For studying too much; you say I should make love,
And that it's having books around me all the time
That gives me bleary eyes and heavy, aching head.

But you don't understand! For this complaint of mine
Comes not from too much reading, nor from midnight oil,
But from the work that keeps me at my desk all day;
And that, ~~That is~~, Pierre my friend, ~~the book~~ I study in.
                  is what

So speak no more of this, if it should be your wish
To give me pleasure, and to irritate me not,
But do instead, while you proceed with skillful hand

To wash my beard and trim my hair to suit my taste,
Just keep me entertained; just tell me, if you will,
Some news about the Pope, and what they say in town.

Joachim DuBellay

* * *

Las où est maintenant ce mespris de Fortune?
Où est ce cœur vainqueur de toute adversité,
Cest honneste desir de l'immortalité,
Et ceste honneste flamme au peuple non commune?

Où sont ces doulx plaisirs, qu'au soir soubs la nuict brune
Les Muses me donnoient, alors qu'en liberté
Dessus le verd tapy d'un rivage esquarté
Je les menois danser aux rayons de la Lune?

Maintenant la Fortune est maistresse de moy,
Et mon cœur qui souloit estre maistre de soi,
Est serf de mille maux et regrets qui m'ennuyent.

De la postérité je n'ay plus de souci,
Ceste divine ardeur, je ne l'ay plus aussi,
Et les Muses de moy, comme estranges, s'enfuyent.

Decay

Alas, where is it now, that fine contempt of Fate?
Where is that heart which conquered all adversity,
That forthright keen desire for immortality,
That upright inner flame, so rare in common men?

Where are those pleasures sweet, which in the dusk of eve
The Muses used to give me, when in spirit free
On some secluded river-bank's lush carpet green,
I used to take them dancing underneath the moon?

Now Fortune has become the mistress of my life;
My heart, which master of itself was wont to be,
Is serf to hordes of vexing troubles and regrets.

No longer do I care about posterity;
That holy ardor also has deserted me,
And the Muses, like shy strangers, from me flee.

* * *

Quand je suis vingt ou trente mois
Sans retourner en Vendômois,
Plein de pensées vagabondes,
Plein d'un remords et d'un souci,
Aux rochers je me plains ainsi,
Aux bois, aux antres et aux ondes.

"Rochers, bien que soyez âgez
De trois mille ans, vous ne changez
Jamais d'état ni de forme;
Mais toujours ma jeunesse fuit,
Et la vieillesse qui me suit
De jeune en vieillard me transforme.

"Bois, bien que perdiez tous les ans
En hiver vos cheveux mouvants,
L'an après qui se renouvelle
Renouvelle aussi votre chef;
Mais le mien ne peut derechef
Revoir sa perruque nouvelle.

"Antres, je me suis vu chez vous
Avoir jadis verts les genoux,
Le corps habile et la main bonne;
Mais ores, j'ai le corps plus dur,
Et les genoux, que ne'est le mur
Qui froidement vous environne.

The Flight of Youth

When I go back to Vendômois,
Where I've not been for months or years,
My mind, beset by vagrant thoughts,
Is filled with troubles, cares, regrets.
Here's how I grumble to the rocks,
The woodlands, caves and little streams:

"O rocks, old friends, though you be aged
Three thousand years, you never change
Your substance nor your form and shape;
But I have changed. My youth has fled,
And Father Time, in hot pursuit,
Transforms me: young man into old.

"O woodlands, though each year you lose
The fickle hair of leaves you wear,
The next year brings it back again,
As good as new; but my bald pate
Cannot so sanguinely expect
To see its vanished wig replaced.

"O caves, when I frequented you,
I used to have good hands, strong arms,
A body lithe, with supple knees;
But now I'm stiff in every joint,
Immobile as the stony walls
That hold you in their cold embrace.

Pierre de Ronsard

"Ondes, sans fin vous promenez
Et vous menez et ramenez
Vos flots d'un cours qui ne séjourne;
Et moi, sans faire long séjour;
Je m'en vais de nuit et de jour
Au lieu d'où plus on ne retourne. . ."

"O streams, your torrents rush along
From place to place, and never stop
Their slow descent toward the sea;
While I, like you, with ne'er a halt,
Keep going, going night and day
Toward the vale of no return. . ."

Pierre de Ronsard

* * *

Mignonne, allons voir si la rose
Qui ce matin avait déclose
Sa robe de pourpre au soleil,
A point perdu cette vêprée
Les plis de sa robe pourprée,
Et son teint au vôtre pareil.

Las! voyez comme en peu d'espace,
Mignonne, elle a dessus la place,
Las! las! ses beautés laissé choir!
O vraiment marâtre Nature,
Puisqu'une telle fleur ne dure
Que du matin jusques au soir!

Donc, si vous me croyez, mignonne,
Tandis que votre âge fleuronne
En sa plus verte nouveauté,
Cueillez, cueillez votre jeunesse:
Comme à cette fleur, la vieillesse
Fera ternir votre beauté.

The Morning-Glory

Mignonne, let's go see if that rose,
Which this morning had just then disclosed
Its imperial hues to the sun,
Still retains, at the close of the day,
'Neath the folds of its bright purple gown,
That complexion so much like your own.

Alas! See how quickly, mignonne,
That poor flower -- alas and alack◗ --
Has just folded its wings and collapsed!
Wicked stepmother Nature, how mean
To have let such a blossom remain
At its best, just from morning 'til eve!

So believe me, take warning, mignonne:
While your beauty's still green, still in bud,
Just beginning to sparkle and glow,
Make the most of it! Take youth and run!
For old age, as the sun did the rose,
Will but tarnish your beauty, anon.

Pierre de Ronsard

* * *

Ah! traistre Amour, donne moy paix ou trêve,
Ou choisissant un autre trait plus fort,
Tranche ma vie, et m'avance la mort;
Douce est la mort d'autant plus qu'elle est brève.

Un soing fecond en mon penser s'éleve,
Qui mon sang hume, et l'esprit me remord,
Et d'Ixion me fait egal au sort,
De qui jamais la peine ne s'acheve.

Que doy-je faire? Amour me fait errer
Si hautement, que je n'ose esperer
De mon salut qu'une langueur extrème.

Puis que mon Dieu ne me veut secourir,
Pour me sauver il me plaist de mourir,
Et de tuer la mort par la mort mesme.

Plea

Ah, traitor Cupid! grant me peace or truce,
Or choose another, stronger arrow now,
Cut short my life, and hasten death for me;
For dying's all the sweeter if it's quick.

A fecund care looms monstrous in my thoughts,
Sucking my blood; my spirit bites and gnaws,
And makes me share the fate of Ixion,
Whose pain and torment never shall be done.

What should I do? Love makes me wander so
In regions high, that I dare not to hope
For any fate save utter languishment.

Since God refuses aid, I must contrive
To save myself, and to that end would die
And kill this living death with death itself.

Pierre de Ronsard

* * *

Je vous envoye un bouquet, que ma main
Vient de tirer de ces fleurs épanies;
Qui ne les eust à ce vespre cueillies,
Cheutes à terre elles fussent demain.

Cela vous soit un exemple certain,
Que vos beautez, bien qu'elles soient fleuries,
En peu de tems cherront toutes fletries,
Et, comme fleurs, periront tout soudain.

Le tems s'en va, le tems s'en va, ma Dame,
Las! le tems non, mais nous nous en allons,
Et tost serons estendus sous la lame,

Et des amours, desquelles nous parlons,
Quand serons morts, n'en sera plus nouvelle:
Pource aimez moy, cependant qu'estes belle.

Flowers

I send you a bouquet, but lately picked
By my own hand from yonder blooming flowers;
Had these not been this evening gathered in,
Tomorrow they'd have fallen to the ground.

Let this for you a certain warning be
That your fair charms, though they be now in bloom,
In no long time will wholly withered droop,
As flowers do, and perish suddenly.

Time passes on, time passes on, madame, —
Alack! Not time — 'tis we who pass away,
And soon shall be laid out beneath the slab;

And of our loves we prattle on about,
When we are dead, the world will speak no more.
So love me now, the while you still are fair.

Pierre de Ronsard

* * *

Quand vous serez bien vieille, au soir, à la chandelle,
Assise auprès du feu, dévidant et filant,
Direz, chantant mes vers, en vous esmerveillant:
"Ronsard me celebroit du temps que j'estois belle."

Lors vous n'aurez servante oyant telle nouvelle,
Desja sous le labeur à demy sommeillant,
Qui au bruit de mon nom ne s'aille resveillant,
Benissant vostre nom de louange immortelle.

Je seray sous la terre, et fantôme sans os;
Par les ombres myrteux je prendray mon repos:
Vous serez au fouyer une vieille accroupie,

Regrettant mon amour et vostre fier desdain.
Vivez, si m'en croyez, n'attendez à demain:
Cueillez dès aujourd'hui les roses de la vie.

To Helen

When you are very old, at eve, by candlelight,
Sitting by the fire to unwind your skein and spin,
You'll sing my verses, and in wonderment will say:
"Ronsard so honored me when I was young and fair."

Then every servant girl of yours, on hearing this,
Thenceforth, though she be half asleep at humdrum toil,
Will rouse herself to listen when she hears my name
And lines that bless your name with everlasting praise.

I'll be beneath the earth, and just a boneless ghost;
In the myrtles' shade I'll be taking my repose;
And you beside the hearth will be a huddled crone

Regretting my lost love and your own proud disdain.
So heed my words, and live; 'wait not tomorrow's dawn,
But pick life's roses now, today, before they're gone.

Pierre de Ronsard

*   *   *

Ces longues nuicts d'hyver, où la Lune ocieuse
Tourne si lentement son char tout à l'entour,
Où le coq si tardif nous annonce le jour,
Où la nuict semble un an à l'âme soucieuse,

Je fusse mort d'ennuy sans ta forme douteuse,
Qui vient par une feinte alleger mon amour,
Et faisant toute nue entre mes bras sejour,
Me pipe doucement d'une joye menteuse.

Vraye tu es farouche, et fiere en cruauté.
De toy fausse on jouyst en toute privauté.
Pres ton mort je m'endors, pres de luy je repose;

Rien ne m'est refusé. Le bon sommeil ainsi
Abuse par le faux mon amoureux souci.
S'abuser en amour n'est pas mauvaise chose.

The Happy Dupe

These long winter nights, when the laggardly Moon
Wheels her chariot so slowly around and about,
When the cock is so tardy announcing the day,
When the night seems a year to the ~~languishing~~ soul,
care-laden
I'd be dead of ennui but for your dreamlike form
Which comes, by some magic, to ease my love-pain,
And by nestling a while fully nude in my arms
Sweetly dupes me, beguiles me with false happiness.

The real you is haughty, and cruelly proud.
One enjoys the false you on terms easy and free.
With your double I doze, find with her sweet repose.

Not a thing is denied me. Thus good, restful sleep
Overcomes by deception my amorous woe.
Self-deception in love a bad thing? I say no.

Le Renard et les raisins

Certain renard gascon, d'autres disent normand,
Mourant presque de faim, vit au haut d'une treille
          Des raisins, mûrs apparemment,
          Et couverts d'une peau vermeille.
Le galant en eût fait volontiers un repas.
          Mais comme il n'y pouvait atteindre,
Ils sont trop verts, dit-il, et bons pour des goujats.

          Fit-il pas mieux que de se plaindre?

The Fox and the Grapes

A certain Gascon* fox — a Norman,* others say —
Was almost starving when, high on an arbor, he
       Espied some grapes, quite plainly ripe,
       Their rosy skins all tight with juice.
Our hero would have liked to make of them a meal,
       But since he could not reach that high,
"They're much too green," said he, "and only good for churls."*

       Was that not better than to whine?

* Since this animal fable seems to be universal and timeless, one might substitute "Texan" and "Yankee" for the two French provincials, and "jerks" for "churls."

Adieux à la vie

Adieu: je vais dans ce pays
D'où ne revint point feu mon père:
Pour jamais adieu, mes amis,
Qui ne me regretterez guère.
Vous en rirez, mes ennemis;
C'est le *requiem* ordinaire.
Vous en tâterez quelque jour;
Et, lorsque aux ténébreux rivages
Vous irez trouver vos ouvrages,
Vous ferez rire à votre tour.

Quand sur la scène de ce monde
Chaque homme a joué son rôlet,
En partant il est à la ronde
Reconduit à coups de sifflet.
Dans leur dernière maladie
J'ai vu des gens de tous états,
Vieux évêques, vieux magistrats,
Vieux courtisans à l'agonie.
Vainement en cérémonie
Avec sa clochette arrivait

L'attirail de la sacristie.
Le curé vainement oignait
Notre vieille âme à sa sortie;
Le public malin s'en moquait;
La satire un moment parlait
Des ridicules de sa vie;
Puis à jamais on l'oubliait:

Farewell to Life

Farewell; I'm going to that land
Whence my late sire did not return.
Goodbye forever, friends of mine,
Who'll scarcely miss me when I'm gone.
And you, my foes, will have a laugh;
That's the familiar *requiem*.
Some day your turn is sure to come,
And when you go to mystic shores
Expecting credit for your works,
You'll raise some laughter in your turn.

When on this world's theatric stage
Each man has played his little role,
He makes his exit to the sound
Of jeers and whistles all around.
I've seen in their last sickness lie
Time-honored men of all estates,
Old courtiers, bishops, magistrates;
I know what happens when they die.
To no avail the ritual,
The ringing of the little bell,

The trappings of the sacristy;
In vain the priest anoints with oil
Our dear departed fellow-soul;
The public mocks him on the sly;
The pen of satire, for a while,
His human foibles ridicules;
Then once for all he is forgot,

Ainsi la farce était finie.
Le purgatoire ou le néant
Terminait cette comédie.

Petits papillons d'un moment,
Invisibles marionnettes,
Qui volez si rapidement
De Polichinelle au néant,
Dites-moi donc ce que vous êtes.
Au terme où je suis parvenu
Quel mortel est le moins à plaindre?
C'est celui qui ne sait rien craindre,
Qui vit et qui meurt inconnu.

And so the farce is at an end.
It's limbo or oblivion
That brings the final curtain down.

O puny, transient butterflies,
Moved puppet-like by unseen strings,
Who flutter off so rapidly
From Punch and Judy to the void,
Just tell me now what else you are.
At this life's term, to which I've come,
What mortal's least to pity here?
It's he who knows no mortal fear,
Who lives his life and dies unsung.

L'Immortalité d'Homère

... Tout s'éteint; les conquérants périssent;
Sur le front des héros les lauriers se flétrissent;
Des antiques cités les débris sont épars;
Sur des remparts détruits s'élèvent des remparts;
L'un par l'autre abattus, les empires s'écroulent;
Les peuples entraînés, tels que les flots qui roulent,
Disparaissent du monde, et les peuples nouveaux
Iront presser les rangs dans l'ombre des tombeaux.
Mais la pensée humaine est l'âme tout entière:
La mort ne détruit pas ce qui n'est point matière:
Le pouvoir absolu s'efforcerait en vain
D'anéantir l'esprit né d'un souffle divin:
Du front de Jupiter c'est Minerve élancée.
Survivant au pouvoir, l'immortelle pensée,
Reine de tous les lieux et de tous les instants,
Traverse l'avenir sur les ailes du Temps.
Brisant des potentats la couronne éphémère,
Trois mille ans ont passé sur la cendre d'Homère,
Et depuis trois mille ans Homère respecté
Est jeune encor de gloire et d'immortalité.

Marie-Joseph Chénier

Homer's Immortality

All things evanesce: conquerors die;
On heroes' brows the laurels wither and decay;
Of ancient cities, only scant debris remains;
On ramparts once destroyed, more ramparts still arise;
Vast empires crumble, overthrown each by the next;
Great peoples strong and skilled, like rolling waves at sea,
Appear and disappear, and each new race will go
To swell the darkling ranks of those who lie entombed.
But human thought's the very essence of the soul;
That which is not material, death does not destroy:
A power absolute would strive but vainly to
Annihilate the mind, born of a breath divine:
From Jupiter's great brow, Minerva springs full-blown.
Outliving earthly power, immortal human thought,
The queen of every clime and every tick of time,
Traverses past and future on the wings of Time.
Three thousand years — enough to break the fleeting crowns
Of potentates — have passed since Homer turned to ash,
And for three thousand years, respected Homer still
Has lived on, ever young, immortalized by fame.

Alfonse de Lamartine

Vers sur un album

Le livre de la vie est le livre suprême
Qu'on ne peut ni fermer, ni rouvrir à son choix;
Le passage attachant ne s'y lit pas deux fois,
Mais le feuillet fatal se tourne de lui-même;
On voudrait revenir à la page où l'on aime
Et la page où l'on meurt est déjà sous vos doigts!

Lines on an Album

a

The book of life's ~~the~~ volume, written and supreme,
That you can't close, and then reopen when you choose;
The gripping passages you can't pause to reread,
But every fated leaf turns over on its own;
You'd like to find again the page where you're in love,
And see beneath your hand the page on which you die!

Extase

J'étais seul près des flots, par une nuit d'étoiles,
Pas un nuage aux cieux, sur les mers pas de voiles.
Mes yeux plongeaient plus loin que le monde réel,
Et les bois, et les monts, et toute la nature
Semblaient interroger dans un confus murmure
        Les flots des mers, les feux du ciel.

Et les étoiles d'or, légions infinies,
A voix haute, à voix basse, avec mille harmonies,
Disaient, en inclinant leurs couronnes de feu;
Et les flots bleus, que rien ne gouverne et n'arrête,
Disaient, en recourbant l'écume de leur crête:
        — C'est le Seigneur, le Seigneur Dieu!

Ecstasy

I was lone by the sea, on a clear, starry night,
Not a cloud in the skies, on the seas not a sail.
My eyes plumbed the vast distance beyond the real world,
And the forests, the hills, all of nature combined
Seemed to interrogate in a murmur obscure
      The sea-waves, the lights in the sky.

And the infinite legions of bright golden stars,
In a whisper, aloud, with a thousand concords,
Seemed to say, tipping humbly their fiery crowns;
And the blue waves, which nothing controls nor arrests,
Seemed to say, bowing down the white foam of their crests:
      "It's the Lord, it's God, the Lord God!"

Victor Hugo

* * *

Lorsque j'étais encore un tout jeune homme pâle,
Et que j'allais entrer dans la lice fatale,
Sombre arène où plus d'un avant moi se perdit,
L'âpre Muse aux regards mystérieux m'a dit:
— Tu pars; mais, quand le Cid se mettait en campagne,
Pour son Dieu, pour son droit et pour sa chère Espagne,
Il était bien armé; ce vaillant Cid avait
Deux casques, deux estocs, sa lance de chevet,
Deux boucliers; il faut des armes de rechange;
Puis il tirait l'épée et devenait archange.
As-tu la dague au flanc? voyons, soldat martyr,
Quelle armure vas-tu choisir et revêtir?
Quels glaives va-t-on voir luire à ton bras robuste?
— J'ai la haine du mal et j'ai l'amour du juste,
Muse; et je suis armé mieux que le paladin.
— Et tes deux boucliers? — J'ai mépris et dédain.

Victor Paratus

When I was a young man still callow and pale
And was planning to enter the pen's fateful lists,
Grim arena where many before me had failed,
The stern Muse with the quizzical gaze said to me:
"Go thou forth; but the Cid, when he launched his campaign
For his God, for his honor, and for his dear Spain,
Was extremely well-armed; that most valiant Cid
Had two helmets, two rapiers, his favorite lance,
And two bucklers; spare arms one must have in advance;
Then he'd draw his great sword and archangel become.
And thou, soldier-martyr? Hast dagger at flank?
What armor wilt thou choose to wear? What bright blades
Shall we see being wielded by thine arm robust?"
— "I have hatred of evil and love of the just,
O Muse; and I'm better than paladins armed."
— "And thy bucklers, the twain?" — "I have scorn and disdain."

Nuits de juin

L'été, lorsque le jour a fui, de fleurs couverte
La plaine verse au loin un parfum enivrant;
Les yeux fermés, l'oreille aux rumeurs entr'ouverte,
On ne dort qu'à demi d'un sommeil transparent.

Les astres sont plus purs, l'ombre paraît meilleure;
Un vague demi-jour teint le dôme éternel;
Et l'aube doux et pâle, en attendant son heure,
Semble toute la nuit errer au bas du ciel.

June Nights

In summer, when the day has fled, the flowered plain
Disperses far and wide a heady redolence;
Eyes closed, ear only just aware of muted sounds,
One drowses in a state of half-transparent sleep.

The stars are purer then, the dark seems more benign;
A kind of twilight tinges heaven's canopy;
And the pale, gentle dawn, awaiting its due time,
Seems all night long to roam about the lower sky.

Victor Hugo

Le Pain Sec

Jeanne était au pain sec dans le cabinet noir,
Pour un crime quelconque, et, manquant au devoir,
J'allai voir la proscrite en pleine forfaiture
Et lui glissai dans l'ombre un pot de confiture
Contraire aux lois. Tous ceux sur qui, dans ma cité,
Repose le salut de la société,
S'indignèrent, et Jeanne a dit d'une voix douce:
"Je ne toucherai plus mon nez avec mon pouce;
Je ne me ferai plus griffer par le minet."
Mais on s'est récrié: "Cette enfant vous connaît;
Elle sait à quel point vous êtes faible et lâche,
Elle vous voit toujours rire quand on se fâche.
Pas de gouvernement possible! A chaque instant
L'ordre est troublé par vous; le pouvoir se détend;
Plus de règle. L'enfant n'a plus rien qui l'arrête.
Vous démolissez tout." – Et j'ai baissé la tête,
Et j'ai dit: "Je n'ai rien à répondre à cela,
J'ai tort. Oui, c'est avec ces indulgences-là
Qu'on a toujours conduit les peuples à leur perte.
Qu'on me mette au pain sec. –Vous le méritez, certe.
On vous y mettra." –Jeanne, alors, dans son coin noir,
M'a dit tout bas, levant ses yeux si beaux à voir,
Pleins de l'autorité des douces créatures:
"Eh bien, moi, je t'irai porter des confitures."

Dry Bread

Joan was on dry bread, shut in a darkened room,
For some atrocious crime, and, shirking duty's call,
I visited the culprit, misdemeanor grave,
And slipped her in the gloom a little jar of jam
Forbid by law. All those on whom, in my abode,
The welfare of society depends, became
Indignant, and Joan said, in soft, pathetic tones:
"I'll never put my thumb up to my nose again;
I'll never make the kitty scratch me any more."
But they expostulated: "That child has you pegged!
She knows how weak and what an easy mark you are;
She always sees you laughing when we frown and scold.
No discipline is possible! At every turn
You flout the rules; you undermine authority.
There's no more rule of law. The child's beyond control.
You're wrecking everything." I hung my head and said:
"I've nothing to reply to that. I'm in the wrong;
And yes, it's true that such indulgences as mine
Have always led to nations' downfall and decay;
So put me on dry bread." "You've earned it, that's for sure.
All right, we will!" Then Joan, whispering in the dark
And looking up at me with those so lovely eyes
Abrim with the assurance of sweet innocents,
Said: "Well then, it's my turn. I'll come and bring you jam."

Après la bataille

Mon père, ce héros au sourire si doux,
Suivi d'un seul housard qu'il aimait entre tous
Pour sa grande bravoure et pour sa haute taille,
Parcourait à cheval, le soir d'une bataille,
Le champ couvert de morts sur qui tombait la nuit.
Il lui sembla dans l'ombre entendre un faible bruit.
C'était un Espagnol de l'armée en déroute
Qui se trainait sanglant sur le bord de la route,
Râlant, brisé, livide, et mort plus qu'à moitié,
Et qui disait: "A boire, à boire, par pitié!"
Mon père, ému, tendit à son housard fidèle
Une gourde de rhum qui pendait à sa selle,
Et dit: "Tiens, donne à boire à ce pauvre blessé."
Tout à coup, au moment où le housard baissé
Se penchait vers lui, l'homme, une espèce de Maure,
Saisit un pistolet qu'il étreignait encore,
Et vise au front mon père en criant: "Caramba!"
Le coup passa si près que le chapeau tomba
Et que le cheval fit un écart en arrière.
"Donne-lui tout de même à boire," dit mon père.

After the Battle

My sire, that mighty hero with the gentle smile,
Attended by his favorite hussar, the one
Loved best for his great courage and his stature tall,
Was riding out across a long day's battlefield
Bestrewn with corpses, just as night began to fall.
Then in the gloom he seemed to hear a muffled sound.
It was a Spanish soldier of the routed force,
Dragging himself along the roadside, trailing blood,
Gasping for breath, all broken, pale, half dead or worse,
And muttering: "A drink! For pity's sake, a drink!"
My father, moved, took from his saddle-bag a gourd
Of rum, and handing it to his faithful hussar,
Said, "Here, give that poor wounded chap a drink of this."
But at the very moment when the hussar bent
Toward him with the gourd, the man, a kind of Moor,
Produced a loaded pistol he was clutching still "*Caramba!*"
And aimed it at my father's head, shouting, ~~Be damned~~ *
The shot just missed, knocking his hat off to the ground
And frightening his horse, which reared and backed away.
"No matter," said my sire. "Go on, give him a drink."

* "Be damned!"

Les Quatre Vents de l'esprit

Je vis les quatre vents passer;
　　　　　　—O vents, leur dis-je,
Vents des cieux! croyez-vous avoir seuls un quadrige?
Autans! masques hagards, tumultueux démons,
Croyez-vous pouvoir seuls aller des mers aux monts?
Croyez-vous seuls pouvoir quitter pour la montagne
Les vagues que l'écume éternelle accompagne,
Fuir, puis, d'un coup de tête effrayant, revenir
A l'ombre où l'on entend ces cavales hennir?
Et vous en retourner soudain, brusques méduses,
Aux cimes dans l'aurore éclatante diffuses,
Et de là crier gloire! aux quatre coins du ciel?
Ces allures d'éclair, ce vol torrentiel,
L'esprit humain les a comme vous, vents tragiques;
Comme vous le printemps, il a ses géorgiques;
Il est l'âcre Archiloque et le Hamlet amer;
Il gonfle l'Iliade ainsi que vous la mer.
L'homme peut de l'abîme effarer la prunelle.
L'âme a comme le ciel quatre souffles en elle;
L'âme a ses pôles; l'âme a ses points cardinaux.
Vents! dragons qui sur nous tordez vos bleus anneaux,
Et qui vous dispersez avec tant de furie
Depuis le hurlement jusqu'à la rêverie,
L'esprit humain n'est pas moins aquilon que vous.
Comme vous il est vie, amour, joie et courroux.
Ses strophes ne sont pas plus vite exténuées
Dans leur vol à travers l'azur que vos nuées;
Un vers court par-dessus les tours et les remparts
Mieux que l'errante bise aux longs cheveux épars;
Et le poète, ouvrant ses intègres registres,

The Four Winds of the Mind

I saw the four winds pass;
                    "O winds," said I to them,
"Sky-sweepers! Do ye think your quadriga unique?
Sea-winds! Untamable, tumultuous afreets,
Think ye that ye alone can go from depths to heights,
That ye alone can quit, for lofty mountain peaks,
The waves of ocean with their everlasting foam,
Can flee, then on an impulse wild, go hurtling back
To that dark realm wherein old Neptune's horses neigh,
And thence return post-haste, abrupt Medusas swift,
To where snow-mantled summits sparkle in the dawn,
And shout God's glory there for all the world to hear?
Those bursts of lightning speed, that wild, torrential flight—
The human mind has them like ye, dramatic winds.
Like ye in spring, it has its zephyrs georgical;
'Tis pungent Archilocus, bitter Hamlet too;
It huffs up Iliads as ye inflate the seas.
The mind of man stares down the eye of the abyss.
The soul, like heaven, has its four prevailing winds;
The soul has its two poles, its four points cardinal.
O winds! ye blue-ringed dragons writhing over us
And with such fervor giving voice throughout the world
In every pitch and tone from shout to reverie,
The human mind is no less versatile than ye.
Like ye, it's all of life: it's love, and joy, and wrath.
Its stanzas, as they soar across the azure vault,
Retain their boundless vigor, like your tireless clouds.
A line of verse can overleap great battlements
With greater ease than can the wild, hirsute North Wind;
The poet, playing his integral registers,

Ne met pas plus de temps que vous, ô vents sinistres,
Pour essuyer sa bouche et changer de clairon.
Comme vous sur la peste, il souffle sur Néron;
Il parle bas aux saints pensifs au fond des grottes;
Il donne une attitude inquiète aux despotes;
La pensée est un aigle à quatre ailes, qui va
Du gouffre où Noé flotte à l'île où Jean rêva;
Et chacun de ses grands ailerons, Epopée,
Drame, Ode, Iambe ardent, coupe comme l'épée;
Le génie a sur lui, dans sa guerre aux fléaux,
Toute l'éclaboussure affreuse du chaos,
Ecume, fange, sang, bave, et pas une tâche.
Il est un et divers. L'idéal se rattache
Comme une croix immense aux quatre angles des cieux.
Le grand char de l'esprit roule sur quatre essieux.
Notre âme, comme vous, ô vents, groupe sonore,
A son nord, son midi, son couchant, son aurore,
Car c'est par la clarté, qu'en ce monde âpre et beau
L'homme finit, son aube étant dans le tombeau.
Le poète est pasteur, juge, prophète, apôtre;
En quatre pas, il peut aller d'un bout à l'autre
De l'art sublime, ainsi que vous de l'horizon;
Et comme vous, s'il est terrible, il a raison;
Sa sagesse et la vôtre ont un air de délire.

L'ombre a tout l'ouragan, l'âme a toute la lyre.

Needs no more time than ye, O sinister great winds,
To wipe his mouth and change his clarion and range.
As ye upon the plague, he blows upon Nero;
He whispers low to pensive saints in grottoes deep;
He makes despots uneasy on their shaky thrones;
His thought is like a four-winged eagle ranging far
From Noah's flooded world to John's dim isle of dreams;
And each of its great pinions, Epic, Drama, Ode
And ardent Iamb, is as trenchant as the sword.
Our genius, in its war on scourges, undergoes
The fearsome spattering of chaos; on it fall
Mad drivel, foam, blood, spittle, filth—and leave no stain.
It is diverse, yet whole. Like a gigantic cross,
Ideals link and bless all corners of the globe.
The mind's great juggernaut rolls on four axles strong.
Like ye, O winds, sonorous roving band, our soul
Has its own north and south, its sunset and its dawn;
For 'tis in light, in this world harsh and beautiful,
That man ends up, his dawn occurring in the tomb.
The poet's shepherd, prophet, judge, apostle too;
In a few steps, he can encompass end to end
His art sublime, as ye the limits of the sky;
And like ye too, though he may terrify, he's wise;
Both his wisdom and yours seem like delirium."

The dark has all the storm; the soul has all the lyre.

Sonnet

Ma vie a son secret, mon âme a son mystère,
Un amour éternel en un moment conçu.
Le mal est sans espoir; aussi j'ai dû le taire
Et celle qui l'a fait n'en a jamais rien su.

Hélas! j'aurai passé près d'elle inaperçu,
Toujours à ses côtés et pourtant solitaire,
Et j'aurai jusqu'au bout fait mon temps sur la terre,
N'osant rien demander et n'ayant rien reçu.

Pour elle, quoique Dieu l'ait faite douce et tendre,
Elle ira son chemin, distraite, et sans entendre
Ce murmure d'amour élevé sur ses pas.

A l'austère devoir pieusement fidèle,
Elle dira, lisant ces vers tout remplis d'elle:
"Quelle est donc cette femme?" et ne comprendra pas.

The Secret

My life its secret has, my soul its mystery:
A love eternal, in one moment realized.
The ache is hopeless; so I've had to hold my tongue,
And she who's caused the pain has never been aware.

Alas! I shall have passed unnoticed close to her,
Forever at her side, yet solitary still,
And shall have spent my time, to my last day on earth,
Not daring aught to ask, not having aught received;

While she, though God made her affectionate and sweet,
Will go her heedless way, sans ever having heard
That murmured sigh of love arising in her wake.

To austere duty piously remaining true,
She'll say, on reading these my verses filled with her:
"Who can that woman be?" and will not see the light.

La Grand'mère

Voici trois ans qu'est morte ma grand'mère
— La bonne femme, — et, quand on l'enterra,
Parents, amis, tout le monde pleura
D'une douleur bien vraie et bien amère.

Moi seul j'errais dans la maison, surpris
Plus que chagrin; et, comme j'étais proche
De son cercueil, — quelqu'un me fit reproche
De voir cela sans larmes et sans cris.

Douleur bruyante est bien vite passée:
Depuis trois ans, d'autres émotions,
Des biens, des maux, — des révolutions, —
Ont dans les coeurs sa mémoire effacée.

Moi seul j'y songe, et la pleure souvent;
Depuis trois ans, par le temps prenant force,
Ainsi qu'un nom gravé dans une écorce,
Son souvenir se creuse plus avant!

Gérard de Nerval

The Grandmother

Three years ago today my grandma died,
— Good woman, she — and when they buried her,
Her relatives and friends and everyone
Shed tears of very real and bitter grief.

I wandered through the house alone, surprised
More than distressed; and as I stood beside
Her coffin — someone asked reproachfully
How I could look, without a tear or cry.

But noisy grief is very quickly spent:
In three years' time, emotions different —
Good luck, misfortune — revolutions too —
Have from all hearts her memory erased.

Alone I think of her, and often weep;
For three years, growing stronger all the while,
Her memory's been deepening its mark,
As does a name carved in a tree's young bark!

Pensée de Byron

Elégie

Par mon amour et ma constance,
J'avais cru fléchir ta rigueur,
Et le souffle de l'espérance
Avait pénétré dans mon coeur;
Mais le temps, qu'en vain je prolonge,
M'a découvert la vérité,
L'espérance a fui comme un songe . . .
Et mon amour seul m'est resté!

Il est resté comme un abîme
Entre ma vie et le bonheur,
Comme un mal dont je suis victime,
Comme un poids jeté sur mon coeur!
Pour fuir le piège où je succombe,
Mes efforts seraient superflus:
Car l'homme a le pied dans la tombe,
Quand l'espoir ne le soutient plus.

J'aimais à réveiller la lyre,
Et souvent, plein de doux transports,
J'osais, ému par le délire,
En tirer de tendres accords.
Que de fois, en versant des larmes,
J'ai chanté tes divins attraits!
Mes accents étaient pleins de charmes,
Car c'est toi qui les inspirais.

Ce temps n'est plus, et le délire
Ne vient plus animer ma voix;

Byronic Thought

Elegy

By love and perfect constancy,
I'd thought to make your rigor yield,
And the sweet breath of living hope
Had penetrated to my heart;
But time, which I prolong in vain,
Has now revealed to me the truth:
That hope has vanished like a dream . . .
And all that's left to me is love!

It has remained like an abyss
Between my life and happiness,
A sickness I'm the victim of,
A crushing weight cast on my heart!
My efforts to escape the trap
In which I'm dying would be vain;
For man has one foot in the grave
When hope has ceased to bear him up.

I used to like to wake the lyre,
And often, filled with rapture sweet,
Would make so bold, by passion stirred,
As tender chords to draw therefrom.
How many times, eyes wet with tears,
I sang of your celestial charms!
My strains to me seemed full of grace
Because by you they were inspired.

That time is gone, and ecstasy
No longer animates my voice;

Je ne trouve point à ma lyre
Les sons qu'elle avait autrefois.
Dans le chagrin qui me dévore,
Je vois mes beaux jours s'envoler;
Si mon oeil étincelle encore,
C'est qu'une larme va couler!

Brisons la coupe de la vie;
Sa liqueur n'est que du poison;
Elle plaisait à ma folie,
Mais elle enivrait ma raison.
Trop longtemps épris d'un vain songe,
Gloire! Amour! vous eûtes mon coeur:
O Gloire! tu n'es qu'un mensonge;
Amour! tu n'es point le bonheur!

I cannot find within my lyre
The sounds it used to make of yore.
With sorrow eating me alive
I see my bright days taking wing;
If my eye sparkles as before,
It's just a tear about to spring!

Let's shatter, then, the cup of life!
Its nectar's but a poison draft;
It's pleased my madness well enough,
But made my reason drunk and daft.
O Glory! Love! Too long ~~you've had~~ *you've had*
My heart enthralled with futile dreams;
O Glory, thou art but a sham!
O Love, thou art not happiness!

Le Roi de Thulé

Il était un roi de Thulé
A qui son amante fidèle
Légua, comme souvenir d'elle,
Une coupe d'or ciselé.

C'était un trésor plein de charmes
Où son amour se conservait:
A chaque fois qu'il y buvait
Ses yeux se remplissaient de larmes.

Voyant ses derniers jours venir,
Il divisa son héritage,
Mais il excepta du partage
La coupe, son cher souvenir.

Il fit à la table royale
Asseoir les barons dans sa tour;
Debout et rangée alentour,
Brillait sa noblesse loyale.

Sous le balcon grondait la mer.
Le vieux roi se lève en silence,
Il boit, — frissonne, et sa main lance
La coupe d'or au flot amer!

Il la vit tourner dans l'eau noire,
La vague en s'ouvrant fit un pli,
Le roi pencha son front pâli . . .
Jamais on ne le vit plus boire.

The King of Thulé

There was a king of far Thulé
To whom his faithful mistress dear
Bequeathed, in memory of her,
A loving cup of graven gold.

It was a treasure full of charms
In which her love was still conserved;
And every time he drank from it,
His eyes would ~~always fill~~ *overflow* with tears.

On seeing his last days draw near,
He made division of his wealth,
But from the sharing held exempt
The cup, his cherished souvenir.

He seated at his royal board
The barons in his terraced tower,
And all around, in bright array,
Stood nobles loyal to his power.

Below the terrace growled the sea.
The old king rises silently,
He drinks, — he trembles, — his hand flings
The gold cup to the briny deep!

In water black he saw it spin;
A wave, in breaking, folded o'er;
The king bent low his ashen brow . . .
He drank thereafter nevermore.

Le Point noir

Quiconque a regardé le soleil fixement
Croit voir devant ses yeux voler obstinément
Autour de lui, dans l'air une tache livide.

Ainsi, tout jeune encore et plus audacieux,
Sur la gloire un instant j'osai fixer les yeux:
Un point noir est resté dans mon regard avide.

Depuis, mêlée à tout comme un signe de deuil,
Partout, sur quelque endroit que s'arrête mon oeil,
Je la vois se poser aussi, la tache noire! —

Quoi, toujours! Entre moi sans cesse et le bonheur!
Oh! c'est que l'aigle seul — malheur à nous! malheur!
Contemple impunément le Soleil et la Gloire.

The Dark Spot

Whoever at the sun has gazed too fixedly
Will think he sees before his eyes, persistently
Flying around him in the air, a livid spot.

So I, still very young and more audacious then,
On glory for a moment dared to fix my eyes:
A dark spot has remained within my avid ken.

Since then, like a mourning-badge ubiquitous,
Whenever, anywhere, my eye may come to rest,
I see it too alight there — that same dark spot!

What, still, without surcease! 'Twixt me and happiness!
It's true! None but the eagle — woe! woe to us all!
Can face the Sun and Glory with impunity.

Notre-Dame de Paris

Notre-Dame est bien vieille: on la verra peut-être
Enterrer cependant Paris qu'elle a vu naître;
Mais, dans quelque mille ans, le Temps fera broncher
Comme un loup fait un bœuf, cette carcasse lourde,
Tordra ses nerfs de fer, et puis d'une dent sourde
Rongera tristement ses vieux os de rocher!

Bien des hommes, de tous les pays de la terre
Viendront, pour contempler cette ruine austère,
Rêveurs, et relisant le livre de Victor;
— Alors ils croiront voir la vieille basilique,
Toute ainsi qu'elle était, puissante et magnifique,
Se lever devant eux comme l'ombre d'un mort!

Notre-Dame de Paris

Notre-Dame is quite old; yet it may well outlive
And bury the Paris it watched being born;
But in some thousand years, Time will bring crashing down,
As a wolf does an ox, that great carcass of stone,
Twisting out its iron sinews, and then with dull teeth
Will gnaw glumly away at its rocky old bones!

Many persons, from countries all over the earth,
Will come to behold that great ruin austere,
Each one pensive, and reading again Victor's book;*
— Then in mind's eye they'll see the basilica old,
At the height of its power and magnificence, rise
Like the ghost of a dead man before their eyes!

* *Notre-Dame de Paris* [The Hunchback of Notre-Dame],
    by Victor Hugo (1831).

Nobles et valets

Ces nobles d'autrefois dont parlent les romans,
Ces preux à front de boeuf, à figures dantesques,
Dont les corps charpentés d'ossements gigantesques
Semblaient avoir au sol racine et fondements;

S'ils revenaient au monde, et qu'il leur prît l'idée
De voir les héritiers de leurs noms immortels,
Race de Laridons, encombrant les hôtels
Des ministres, — rampante, avide et dégradée;

Etres grêles, à buscs, plastrons et faux mollets: —
Certes, ils comprendraient alors, ces nobles hommes,
Que, depuis les vieux temps, au sang de gentilshommes
Leurs filles ont mêlé bien du sang de valets!

Nobles and Lackeys

Those legendary noblemen of yesteryear,
Those valiant champions, ox-browed, Dantesque of mien,
Whose bodies huge, rough-hewn and powerful appeared
To have their roots established firmly in the ground;

Should they come back to life, and take a notion to
Observe the present heirs to their immortal names,
A race of Laridons,* encumbering the halls
Of ministries — greedy, obsequious, debased

Weaklings with padded calves, corsets and dickeys —
Then certainly those noble men would understand:
Since olden times, the daughters of great gentlemen
Have mixed their blood with that of many lackeys!

* Laridons: degenerates. "Nincompoops" is a tempting alternative.

Avril

Déjà les beaux jours, la poussière,
Un ciel d'azur et de lumière,
Les murs enflammés, les longs soirs;
Et rien de vert: à peine encore
Un reflet rougeâtre décore
Les grands arbres aux rameaux noirs!

Ce beau temps me pèse et m'ennuie.
Ce n'est qu'après des jours de pluie
Que doit surgir, en un tableau,
Le printemps verdissant et rose,
Comme une nymphe fraîche éclose,
Qui, souriante, sort de l'eau.

April

Now sunny days, dust in the air,
A sky of azure and of light,
The walls on fire, long afternoons,
And nothing green; the merest trace
Of reddish haze as yet adorns
The big trees with their black boughs bare!

I chafe at such clear April skies.
'Tis not 'til after days of rain
That lovely pink and greening Spring
Will burgeon forth in one tableau,
Like one full-blown, fresh water-nymph
Emerging, smiling, from below.

Le Réveil en voiture

Voici ce que je vis: Les arbres sur ma route
Fuyaient mêlés, ainsi qu'une armée en déroute,
Et sous moi, comme ému par les vents soulevés,
Le sol roulait des flots de glèbe et de pavés!

Des clochers conduisaient parmi les plaines vertes
Leurs hameaux aux maisons de plâtre, recouvertes
En tuiles, qui trottaient ainsi que des troupeaux
De moutons blancs, marqués en rouge sur le dos!

Et les monts enivrés chancelaient, — la rivière
Comme un serpent boa, sur la vallée entière
Etendu, s'élançait pour les entortiller . . .
— J'étais en poste, moi, venant de m'éveiller!

Waking Up on a Coach

Now this is what I saw: The trees along my route
Were rushing off in disarray, like routed troops,
And under me the ground, as if stirred up by winds,
Was like a heaving sea of clods and paving-stones!

The spires of churches led among the verdant ~~plains~~ *fields*
Their villages of plaster houses roofed with tile,
Which trotted after them like flocks of docile sheep
As white as snow, with markings on their backs in red!

The drunken hills were staggering — the river, like
A boa writhing down the valley all the way,
Was lashing out to coil itself around them all . . .
— I was on the mail coach, and had just come awake!

Le Relais

En voyage, on s'arrête, on descend de voiture;
Puis entre deux maisons on passe à l'laventure
Des chevaux, de la route et des fouets étourdi,
L'oeil fatigué et le corps engourdi.

Et voici tout à coup, silencieuse et verte,
Une vallée humide et de lilas couverte,
Un ruisseau qui murmure entre les peupliers, —
Et la route et le bruit sont bien vite oubliés!

On se couche dans l'herbe et l'on s'écoute vivre,
De l'odeur du foin vert à loisir on s'enivre,
Et sans penser à rien on regarde les cieux . . .
Hélas! une voix crie: "En voiture, messieurs!"

The Coach-Stop

In mid-journey, we stop; one alights from the coach,
Then at random strolls out between houses, bemused,
In a daze from the horses, the highway, the whips,
Eyes smarting and tired, body stiff and benumbed.

And then all of a sudden, here, quiet and green,
Is a moist, fertile valley, with lilacs in bloom,
A brook gurgling down between cool poplar trees,
And the road and its din are forgotten with ease!

One lies down in the grass, listens to himself live,
Gets as drunk as he likes on the smell of green hay,
And thinking of nothing, looks up at the sky . . .
Alas! A voice cries: "All aboard, gentlemen!"

Fantaisie

Il est un air pour qui je donnerais
Tout Rossini, tout Mozart, tout Wéber,
Un air très vieux, languissant et funèbre,
Qui pour moi seul a des charmes secrets!

Or, chaque fois que je viens à l'entendre,
De deux cents ans mon âme rajeunit . . .
C'est sous Louis Treize; et je crois voir s'étendre
Un coteau vert, que le couchant jaunit.

Puis un château de brique à coins de pierre,
Aux vitraux teints de rougeâtres couleurs,
Ceint de grands parcs, avec une rivière
Baignant ses pieds, qui coule entre les fleurs.

Puis une dame, à sa haute fenêtre,
Blonde aux yeux noirs, en ses habits anciens,
Que, dans une autre existence, peut-être,
J'ai déjà vue . . . et dont je me souviens!

Fantasy

There is a melody for which I'd give
All Mozart, all Rossini, all Weber,
An old, old tune, mournful and languishing,
Which has for me alone some secret charms!

Now every time I chance to hear it played,
My soul grows younger by two hundred years;
It's Louis Treize's time; I seem to see
A hillside green, turned gold by setting sun.

Then a chateau, of brick with quoins of stone,
Its stained-glass windows tinted reddish hues,
Surrounded by broad parklands, with a stream
To bathe its feet, flowing between parterres.

And then a lady, at her casement high,
Fair-haired, dark-eyed, in antique raiment clad,
Whom I, in some anterior life, perhaps,
Have seen before . . . and whom I can't forget!

Laisse-moi!

Non, laisse-moi, je t'en supplie;
En vain, si jeune et si jolie,
Tu voudrais ranimer mon coeur:
Ne vois-tu pas, à ma tristesse,
Que mon front pâle et sans jeunesse
Ne doit plus sourire au bonheur?

Qund l'hiver aux froides haleines
Des fleurs qui brillent dans nos plaines
Glace le sein épanoui,
Qui peut rendre à la feuille morte
Ses parfums que la brise emporte
Et son éclat évanoui!

O! si je t'avais rencontrée
Alors que mon âme enivrée
Palpitait de vie et d'amours,
Avec quel transport, quel délire
J'aurais accueilli ton sourire
Dont le charme eût nourri mes jours.

Mais à present, ô jeune fille!
Ton regard, c'est l'astre qui brille
Aux yeux troublés des matelots
Dont la barque en proie au naufrage,
A l'instant où cesse l'orage
Se brise et s'enfuit sous les flots.

Leave Me!

No, leave me, please, I beg of you!
In vain, so young and pretty, you
Would animate my heart again.
Does not my sadness make you see
That my pale brow, no longer young,
Will glow no more with happiness?

When winter with its frigid breath
Congeals the open, blooming hearts
Of sparkling flowers in our fields,
Who can restore to blossoms dead
Their perfume wafted on the breeze
And their now-faded brilliancy?

Oh! had I met you long ago
When my inebriated soul
Was all athrob with life and loves,
With what delirious rapture I
Would then have welcomed your sweet smile,
Which would have nourished all my days!

But now, today, O pretty miss!
Your glance is like the sun that shines
In shipwrecked sailors' dazzled eyes
While their storm-battered, stricken ship,
Just as the storm subsides at last,
Breaks up and sinks beneath the waves.

Gérard de Nerval

Non, laisse-moi, je t'en supplie;
En vain, si jeune et si jolie,
Tu voudrais ranimer mon coeur:
Sur ce front pâle et sans jeunesse
Ne vois-tu pas que la tristesse,
A banni l'espoir du bonheur?

No, leave me, please, I beg of you!
In vain, so young and pretty, you
Would animate my heart again.
On this pale brow, no longer young,
Can you not see, despondency
Has banished hope of happiness?

Vers Dorés

Eh quoi! tout est sensible!
Pythagoras

Homme! libre penseur — te crois-tu seul pensant
Dans ce monde où la vie éclate en toute chose?
Des forces que tu tiens ta liberté dispose,
Mais de tous tes conseils l'univers est absent.

Respecte dans la bête un esprit agissant: . . .
Chaque fleur est une âme à la Nature éclose;
Un mystère d'amour dans le métal repose:
"Tout est sensible!" Et tout sur ton être est puissant.

Crains, dans le mur aveugle un regard qui t'épie:
A la matière même un verbe est attaché . . .
Ne la fais pas servir à quelque usage impie!

Souvent dans l'être obscur habite un Dieu caché;
Et comme un oeil naissant couvert par ses paupières,
Un pur esprit s'accroît sous l'écorce des pierres!

Golden Verses

Eh quoi! tout est sensible!
Pythagoras

O free, thinking Man! do you think all alone
In this world where there's life bursting forth in all things?
You may freely dispose of the powers that you have,
But you take no account of the non-human world.

Respect in the beast active spirit and mind; . . .
Every flower is a soul, in great Nature abloom;
A miracle-play in cold metal abides.
"All is sentient!" — and all has effect on your being.

Beware, in blind walls there's a gaze watching you.
Inert matter itself has a power of speech . . .
Do not use it to serve any impious end!

In a creature obscure, hidden God often dwells;
And like a nascent eye screened from sight by its lids,
A pure spirit swells 'neath the hard crust of stones!

Epitaphe

Il a vécu tantôt gai comme un sansonnet
Tour à tour amoureux insoucieux et tendre,
Tantôt sombre et rêveur comme un triste Clitandre;
Un jour il entendit qu'à sa porte on sonnait.

C'était la Mort! Alors il la pria d'attendre
Qu'il eût posé le point à son dernier sonnet;
Et puis sans s'émouvoir, il s'en alla s'étendre
Au fond du coffre froid où son corps frissonnait.

Il était paresseux, à ce que dit l'histoire,
Il laissait trop sécher l'encre dans l'écritoire.
Il voulait tout savoir mais il n'a rien connu.

Et quand vint le moment où, las de cette vie,
Un soir d'hiver, enfin l'âme lui fut ravie,
Il s'en alla disant: "Pourquoi suis-je venu?"

Epitaph

He lived his life at times as ~~gay as any lark~~ *Gay as any lark,*
A carefree, tender lover, yet at times, by turns,
A melancholy dreamer, like a sad Clitandre;
One day he heard the sound of someone at his door.

'Twas Death! He begged it wait a moment, while he put
A period to his sonnet, this his very last;
And then, without a qualm, away he went to lay
His quaking body out within the coffin cold.

He was, the story goes, a lazy fellow who
Too often let the ink within the inkwell dry;
He sought to know all things, but nothing did he learn.

And when at last, one winter's eve, the moment came
When, weary of this life, his soul was snatched away,
His last words in departing were: "Why did I come?"

Stances élégiaques

Ce ruisseau, dont l'onde tremblante
Réfléchit la clarté des cieux,
Paraît dans sa course brillante
Etinceler de mille feux;
Tandis qu'au fond du lit paisible,
Où, par une pente insensible,
Lentement s'écoulent ses flots,
Il entraîne une fange impure
Qui d'amertume et de souillure
Partout empoisonne ses eaux.

De même un passager délire,
Un éclair rapide et joyeux
Entr'ouvre ma bouche au sourire
Et la gaîté brille en mes yeux;
Cependant mon âme est de glace,
Et rien n'effacera la trace
Des malheurs qui m'ont terrassé.
En vain passera ma jeunesse,
Toujours l'importune tristesse
Gonflera mon cœur oppressé.

Car il est un nuage sombre,
Un souvenir mouillé de pleurs,
Qui m'accable et répand son ombre
Sur mes plaisirs et mes douleurs.
Dans ma profonde indifférence,

Elegiac Stanzas

This little brook, whose rippling wave
Reflects the brightness of the skies,
Appears to sparkle in its course
With light as of a thousand fires;
While on the quiet bed below,
An incline imperceptible
Down which its waters slowly flow,
It drags along some rotten filth
Whose bitter taste and ugly stain
Pollute its waters through and through.

Just so, a momentary joy,
A random, fleeting, happy thought,
Will bend my mouth to half a smile
And bring a twinkle to my eye.
My soul, however, is of ice,
And nothing will efface the mark
Of sorrows that have laid me low.
In vain my youth will pass away,
And melancholy importune
Will still oppress my swollen heart.

For there's a somber, murky cloud,
A memory wet with bitter tears,
That overwhelms me, casting down
Its shadow on my weal and woe.
In my profound indifference,

De la joie ou de la souffrance
L'aiguillon ne peut m'émouvoir;
Les biens que le vulgaire envie
Peut-être embelliront ma vie,
Mais rien ne me rendra l'espoir.

Du tronc à demi détachée
Par le souffle des noirs autans,
Lorsque la branche desséchée
Revoit les beaux jours du printemps,
Si parfois un rayon mobile,
Errant sur sa tête stérile,
Vient brillanter ses rameaux nus,
Elle sourit à la lumière;
Mais la verdure printanière
Sur son front ne renaîtra plus.

No stimulus of joy or pain
Can deeply move or stir my soul;
Good things by others coveted
May lend some beauty to my life,
But naught to me will hope restore.

The withered branch that wintry winds
Have halfway severed from the trunk,
When it sees once again return
The lovely days of spring, if now
And then an errant ray of sun
Descends upon its barren head
And sets its naked twigs agleam,
The branch may smile to see the light,
But on its brow, the green of spring
Will never be reborn again.

Gérard de Nerval

Mélodie irlandaise*

Le soleil du matin commençait sa carrière,
Je vis près du rivage une barque légère
Se bercer mollement sur les flots argentés.
Je revins quand la nuit descendait sur la rive:
La nacelle était là, mais l'onde fugitive
Ne baignait plus ses flancs dans le sable arrêtés.

Et voilà notre sort! au matin de la vie
Par des rêves d'espoir notre âme poursuivie
Se balance un moment sur les flots du bonheur;
Mais, sitôt que le soir étend son voile sombre,
L'onde qui nous portait se retire, et dans l'ombre
Bientôt nous restons seuls en proie à la douleur.

Au déclin de nos jours on dit que notre tête
Doit trouver le repos sous un ciel sans tempête;
Mais qu'importe à mes vœux le calme de la nuit!
Rendez-moi le matin, la fraîcheur et les charmes;
Car je préfère encor ses brouillards et ses larmes
Aux plus douces lueurs du soleil qui s'enfuit.

Oh! qui n'a désiré voir tout à coup renaître
Cet instant dont le charme éveilla dans son être
Et des sens inconnus et de nouveaux transports!
Où son âme, semblable à l'écorce embaumée
Qui disperse en brûlant sa vapeur parfumée,
Dans les feux de l'amour exhala ses trésors!

* Authorship now in question

Irish Melody

As the sun one fine morning began its career,
I remarked near the shore a light-hulled little boat
Rocking gently at anchor, on shimmering waves.
I returned just as dusk was descending on shore.
The skiff was still there, but in sand high and dry,
Its sides washed no more by the fugitive tide.

That's the fate we all share! In the morning of life
Our soul, all enrapt in our bright, hopeful dreams,
Rides at ease for a while on the flood-tide of joy;
But no sooner does evening deploy its dark veil
Than the upbearing waters recede, and ere long
We are left all alone in the dark, prey to pain.

People say that we shall, at the close of our days,
Find repose for our heads, under skies clear of storms.
But what good to my dreams is the night's vaunted calm?
O give me back morning, its freshness and charms!
I prefer all its fogginess, all its salt tears,
To the sweetest bright gleams of the sun going down.

Ah, who has not longed to relive suddenly
That magical moment when in him first stirred
Strange new feelings and transports of spirit and sense!
When his soul, like the bark of a sandalwood tree
Which in burning disperses its incense abroad,
In the fires of first love its rich treasures exhaled!

Molière

J'étais seul, l'autre soir, au Théâtre-Français,
Ou presque seul; l'auteur n'avait pas grand succès.
Ce n'était que Molière, et nous savons de reste
Que ce grand maladroit, qui fit un jour Alceste,
Ignora le bel art de chatouiller l'esprit
Et de servir à point un dénouement bien cuit.
Grâce à Dieu, nos auteurs ont changé de méthode,
Et nous aimons bien mieux quelque drame à la mode,
Où l'intrigue, enlacée et roulée en feston,
Tourne comme un rébus autour d'un mirliton.
J'écoutais cependant cette simple harmonie,
Et comme le bon sens fait parler le génie.
J'admirais quel amour pour l'âpre vérité
Eut cet homme si fier en sa naïveté,
Quel grand et vrai savoir des choses de ce monde,
Quelle mâle gaîté, si triste et si profonde,
Que, lorsqu'on vient d'en rire, on devrait en pleurer!
Et je me demandais: "Est-ce assez d'admirer?
Est-ce assez de venir, un soir, par aventure,
D'entendre au fond de l'âme un cri de la nature,
D'essuyer une larme, et de partir ainsi,
Quoi qu'on fasse d'ailleurs, sans en prendre souci?
Puis je songeais encore (ainsi va la pensée)
Que l'antique franchise, à ce point délaissée,
Avec notre finesse et notre esprit moqueur,
Ferait croire, après tout, que nous manquons de coeur;
Que c'était une triste et honteuse misère
Que cette solitude à l'entour de Molière,
Et qu'il est *pourtant temps*, comme dit la chanson,

Alfred de Musset

Molière

I sat, the other night, in the Théâtre-Français
Alone, or nearly so; the play was not a hit.
'Twas only Molière, and we know all too well
That that great maladroit, creator of Alceste,
Knew nothing of the art of titillating wit
And serving up *à point* a well-done denouement.
Thank goodness, playwrights now have changed the way they write,
And we prefer a modern, stylish kind of play
Whose plot, threads intertwined and rolled up in festoon,
Is like a rebus wound around a whirligig.
But what I heard that night was simple harmony
And common sense, expressed as only genius can.
I marveled what a love for speaking bitter truth
That man, so proud in all his naïveté, possessed;
What vast, true understanding of this world's affairs;
What virile comedy, so sad and so profound
That even as one laughs, he feels he ought to weep!
I asked myself: "Is it enough, just to admire?
Is it enough to come, one night by happenstance,
To hear within one's soul a cry of human pain,
To wipe away a tear, to leave, and then to go
About one's own affairs without a further care?
Then this occurred to me (so goes the train of thought):
That our abandonment of candor as *passé*,
Our preference for subtle wit and mockery,
Would argue, after all, that we are lacking heart;
That all the solitude around Molière that night
Was nothing less than sorry, shameful travesty;
And that it's now *high time*, as they say in the song,

De sortir de ce siècle ou d'en avoir raison.
Car à quoi comparer cette scène embourbée
Et l'effroyable honte où la muse est tombée?
La lâcheté nous bride, et les sots vont disant
Que, sous ce vieux soleil, tout est fait à présent;
Comme si les travers de la famille humaine
Ne rajeunissaient pas chaque an, chaque semaine.
Notre siècle a ses moeurs, partant sa vérité;
Celui qui l'ose dire est toujours écouté.
Ah! j'oserais parler, si je croyais bien dire.
J'oserais ramasser le fouet de la satire,
Et l'habiller de noir, cet homme aux rubans verts,
Qui se fâchait jadis pour quelques mauvais vers.
S'il rentrait aujourd'hui dans Paris, la grand'ville,
Il y trouverait mieux, pour émouvoir sa bile,
Qu'une méchante femme et qu'un méchant sonnet;
Nous avons autre chose à mettre au cabinet.
O notre maître à tous! si ta tombe est fermée,
Laisse-moi dans ta cendre, un instant ranimée
Trouver une étincelle, et je vais t'imiter!
J'en aurai fait assez si je puis le tenter.
Apprends-moi de quel ton, dans ta bouche hardie,
Parlait la vérité, ta seule passion;
Et pour me faire entendre, à défaut du génie,
J'en aurai le courage et l'indignation.

To get out of this age, or make some sense of it!
For what's to be compared with our bemired stage,
With the disgraceful state the muse has fallen to?
We're bridled by our fears, and fools are saying that
Beneath this ancient sun, all things have now been done,
—As if the failings of the human family
Don't manifest themselves anew each year, each week!
Our era has its moral tone, and so its truth;
Whoever dares to tell that truth will still be heard.
Had I the eloquence, I'd speak to this myself!
I'd boldly take in hand the whip of satire keen
And dress in black that fellow with the ribbons green,
Whom some bad verses made so angry long ago.
Were he to come today to "Paris, la grand'ville,"
He'd find more potent things to stimulate his bile
Than a malicious woman and a sonnet vile;
We've other things to put in the collection-case.
O mentor of us all! Though you be long entombed,
Let me find in your ashes but a single spark
Revived for just an instant, and I'll echo you!
I shall have done enough if I can only try.
Teach me the tone in which, from out your mouth so bold,
Held forth the voice of truth, your only passion;
And to make sure I'm heard, in lieu of genius,
I'll have its courage and its indignation.

Rôle moral de la Douleur
(C'est la Muse qui parle)

Si l'effort est trop grand pour la faiblesse humaine
De pardonner les maux qui nous viennent d'autrui,
Epargne-toi du moins le tourment de la haine;
A défaut du pardon, laisse venir l'oubli.
Les morts dorment en paix dans le sein de la terre;
Ainsi doivent dormir nos sentiments éteints.
Ces reliques du coeur ont aussi leur poussière;
Sur leurs restes sacrés ne portons pas les mains.
Pourquoi, dans ce récit d'une vive souffrance,
Ne veux-tu voir qu'un rêve et qu'un amour trompé?
Est-ce donc sans motif qu'agit la Providence?
Et crois-tu donc distrait le Dieu qui t'a frappé?
Le coup dont tu te plains t'a préservé peut-être,
Enfant; car c'est par là que ton coeur s'est ouvert.
L'homme est un apprenti, la douleur est son maître,
Et nul ne se connaît, tant qu'il n'a pas souffert.
C'est une dure loi, mais une loi suprême,
Vieille comme le monde et la fatalité,
Qu'il nous faut du malheur recevoir le baptême,
Et qu'à ce triste prix tout doit être acheté.
Les moissons, pour mûrir, ont besoin de rosée;
Pour vivre et pour sentir, l'homme a besoin des pleurs;
La joie a pour symbole une plante brisée,
Humide encor de pluie et couverte de fleurs.
Ne te disais-tu pas guéri de ta folie?
N'es-tu pas jeune, heureux, partout le bienvenu?
Et ces plaisirs légers qui font aimer la vie,
Si tu n'avais pleuré, quel cas en ferais-tu?

Alfred de Musset

The Moral Role of Pain
(the Muse speaking)

If human weakness makes the effort just too great
For thee to pardon all ~~the troubles inflictions~~ *thy woes by others*
wrought,
At least have mercy on thyself: let rancor die.
If thou canst not forgive, let go, and just forget.
The dead repose in peace within the breast of earth;
Our feelings, once extinguished, ought to sleep so too.
Those relics of the heart also leave dust behind;
So let's not lay our hands on sanctified remains.
Why shouldst thou see, in this account of painful grief,
Only a shattered dream, an unrequited love?
Does Providence just act, sans motive or intent?
Was God distracted when He wrongly struck thee down?
The blow thou suffered may have saved the child thou wert;
It may have been that blow which opened wide thy heart.
Man is apprenticed to the master-teacher Pain,
And no man knows himself, until he's suffered woe.
This is the law—a harsh law, yes, but still supreme
And ancient as the human world and fate itself:
That we must undergo baptism of mischance,
And at that painful price must pay for everything.
All growing crops, to ripen, need the dew and rain;
To be alive and sentient, man has need of tears;
Symbolic of great joy is a storm-ravaged plant
Still wet with rain and covered with a mass of bloom.
Wert thou not heard to say, thy madness now is cured?
Art thou not young, well-favored, welcome everywhere?
And simple pleasures that make life so dear to us—
What would they mean to thee, if thou hadst never wept?

Lorsqu'au déclin du jour, assis sur la bruyère,
Avec un vieil ami tu bois en liberté,
Dis-moi, d'aussi bon coeur lèverais-tu ton verre,
Si tu n'avais senti le prix de la gaîté?
Aimerais-tu les fleurs, les prés et la verdure,
Les sonnets de Pétrarque et le chant des oiseaux,
Michel-Ange et les arts, Shakespeare et la nature,
Si tu n'y retrouvais quelques anciens sanglots?
Comprendrais-tu des cieux l'ineffable harmonie,
Le silence des nuits, le murmure des flots,
Si quelque part là-bas la fièvre et l'insomnie
Ne t'avaient fait songer à l'éternel repos?
De quoi te plains-tu donc? L'immortelle espérance
S'est retrempée en toi sous la main du malheur.
Pourquoi veux-tu haïr ta jeune expérience
Et détester un mal qui t'a rendu meilleur?...

When at the close of day thou sittest on the green
To drink with some old friend, in leisure and at ease,
Now tell me, wouldst thou raise thy glass so heartily
If thou hadst never learned the price of gaiety?
Wouldst thou love flowers, fields and springtime greenery,
The sonnets of Petrarch, the lilting songs of birds,
Art and Michelangelo, nature and Shakespeare,
Foundest thou not ~~therein~~ reminders of past sobs? *therein*
Wouldst thou perceive the heavens' wondrous harmony
The silence of the night, the murmur of the sea,
If somewhere in the past, fever and sleeplessness
Had not led thee to contemplate eternal rest?
So why shouldst thou complain? Immortal Hope, in thee,
Beneath the hand of Pain has braced itself anew.
Why then shouldst thou detest thy youth's experience
And hate a woe that's made of thee a better man?

Au Lecteur

La sottise, l'erreur, le péché, la lésine,
Occupent nos esprits et travaillent nos corps,
Et nous alimentons nos aimables remords,
Comme les mendiants nourrissent leur vermine.

Nos péchés sont têtus, nos repentirs sont lâches;
Nous nous faisons payer grassement nos aveux,
Et nous rentrons gaiement dans le chemin bourbeux,
Croyant par de vils pleurs laver toutes nos taches.

Sur l'oreiller du mal c'est Satan Trismégiste
Qui berce longuement notre esprit enchanté,
Et le riche métal de notre volonté
Est tout vaporisé par ce savant chimiste.

C'est le Diable qui tient les fils qui nous remuent!
Aux objets répugnants nous trouvons des appas;
Chaque jour vers l'Enfer nous descendons d'un pas,
Sans horreur, à travers des ténèbres qui puent.

Ainsi qu'un débauché pauvre qui baise et mange
Le sein martyrisé d'une antique catin,
Nous volons au passage un plaisir clandestin
Que nous pressons bien fort comme une vieille orange.

Serré, fourmillant, comme un million d'helminthes,
Dans nos cerveaux ribote un peuple de Démons,
Et, quand nous respirons, la Mort dans nos poumons
Descend, fleuve invisible, avec de sourdes plaintes.

Charles Baudelaire

To the Reader

Stupidity, selfishness, error and sin
Belabor our bodies and prey on our minds,
And we lovingly feed our regrets and remorse
As verminous mendicants nurture their lice.

Our sins are ingrained, our repentances lax;
We exact for confessions a handsome reward,
And we blithely return to the path through the mire,
Expecting cheap tears to wash out all our stains.

On the pillow of evil it's Satan Thrice Great
Who constantly cradles our spirit enthralled,
And the metal, the strong tempered steel of our will
By that masterful chemist is turned into dust.

When we move, it's the Devil who's pulling the strings!
In the most loathsome things we discover some charm;
Every day we descend one more step toward Hell
Through a darkness that stinks, without horror or qualm.

Like an indigent lecher who kisses and bites
The martyrized breast of an elderly whore,
We casually steal some clandestine delight,
Which we squeeze very hard like a shriveled old orange.

Packed tightly and swarming like millions of worms,
A host of foul Demons carouse in our brains,
And whenever we breathe, Death flows down to our lungs,
An invisible river, with dull, hollow moans.

Si le viol, le poison, le poignard, l'incendie,
N'ont pas encor brodé de leurs plaisants dessins
Le canevas banal de nos piteux destins,
C'est que notre âme, hélas! n'est pas assez hardie.

Mais parmi les chacals, les panthères, les lices,
Les singes, les scorpions, les vautours, les serpents,
Les monstres glapissants, hurlants, grognants, rampants,
Dans la ménagerie infâme de nos vices,

Il en est un plus laid, plus méchant, plus immonde!
Quoiqu'il ne pousse ni grands gestes ni grands cris,
Il ferait volontiers de la terre un débris
Et dans un bâillement avalerait le monde;

C'est l'Ennui! — l'œil chargé d'un pleur involontaire,
Il rêve d'échafauds en fumant son houka.
Tu le connais, lecteur, ce monstre délicat,
— Hypocrite lecteur, — mon semblable, — mon frère!

If poisoning, fire-setting, stabbing and rape
Have not yet embroidered their striking designs
On the drab counterpane of our pitiful lives,
It's just that, alas, we're too timid of soul!

But among the hyenas, the panthers, the hounds,
The monkeys, the scorpions, the vultures, the snakes,
All the slavering monsters that yap, howl and roar
In the infamous zoo of our vices, there's one

That is ugliest, filthiest, meanest of all!
Though it's sluggish of movement and utters no cries,
It would willingly make of the earth mere debris,
And would swallow the world in a single great yawn;

It's Ennui! — With an unconscious tear in its eye
And smoking its hookah, of gallows it dreams.
You know it, O reader, this monster effete,
— Hypocritical reader — my fellow — my twin!

Bénédiction

Lorsque, par un décret des puissances suprêmes,
Le Poëte apparaît en ce monde ennuyé,
Sa mère épouvantée et pleine de blasphèmes
Crispe ses poings vers Dieu, qui la prend en pitié:

—"Ah! que n'ai-je mis bas tout un nœud de vipères,
Plutôt que de nourrir cette dérision!
Maudite soit la nuit aux plaisirs éphémères
Où mon ventre a conçu mon expiation!

Puisque tu m'as choisie entre toutes les femmes
Pour être le dégoût de mon triste mari,
Et que je ne puis pas rejeter dans les flammes,
Comme un billet d'amour, ce monstre rabougri,

Je ferai rejaillir ta haine qui m'accable
Sur l'instrument maudit de tes méchancetés,
Et je tordrai si bien cet arbre misérable,
Qu'il ne pourra pousser ses boutons empestés!"

Elle ravale ainsi l'écume de sa haine,
Et, ne comprenant pas les desseins éternels,
Elle-même prépare au fond de la Géhenne
Les bûchers consacrés aux crimes maternels.

Pourtant, sous la tutelle invisible d'un Ange,
L'Enfant déshérité s'enivre de soleil,
Et dans tout ce qu'il boit et dans tout ce qu'il mange
Retrouve l'ambroisie et le nectar vermeil.

Benediction

When, by some decree of the powers that be,
The Poet appears in this bored, weary world,
His mother, dismayed and with blasphemy filled,
Shakes her clenched fist at God, who takes pity on her:

"Ah, would I had borne a great tangle of snakes,
Rather than nurture this travesty vile!
Accursed be that night with its transient delights
When my belly conceived my atonement for sin!

Since of all the world's women you've singled out me
To fill my poor husband with grief and disgust,
And I can't throw this misshapen monster away,
As I would a love-letter, into the fire,

I shall turn all your hatred that overwhelms me
On the damned instrument of your malice and spite,
And so hard shall I twist this contemptible tree
That it never can put forth its foul, stinking buds!"

Thus she chokes back and swallows the foam of her hate,
And, not understanding the eternal designs,
By her own hand prepares in Gehenna's dark depths
The pyres dedicated to motherly crimes.

Nonetheless, in an Angel's invisible charge,
The derelict Child imbibes sunshine like wine,
And in all that he eats and in all that he drinks
Finds ambrosia and nectar like that of the gods.

Il joue avec le vent, cause avec le nuage,
Et s'enivre en chantant du chemin de la croix;
Et l'Esprit qui le suit dans son pèlerinage
Pleure de le voir gai comme un oiseau des bois.

Tous ceux qu'il veut aimer l'observent avec crainte,
Ou bien, s'enhardissant de sa tranquillité,
Cherchent à qui saura lui tirer une plainte,
Et font sur lui l'essai de leur férocité.

Dans le pain et le vin destinés à sa bouche
Ils mêlent de la cendre avec d'impurs crachats;
Avec hypocrisie ils jettent ce qu'il touche,
Et s'accusent d'avoir mis leurs pieds dans ses pas.

Sa femme va criant sur les places publiques:
"Puisqu'il me trouve assez belle pour m'adorer,
Je ferai le métier des idoles antiques,
Et comme elles je veux me faire redorer;

Et je me soûlerai de nard, d'encens, de myrrhe,
De génuflexions, de viandes et de vins,
Pour savoir si je puis dans un cœur qui m'admire
Usurper en riant les hommages divins!

Et, quand je m'ennuierai de ces farces impies,
Je poserai sur lui ma frêle et forte main;
Et mes ongles, pareils aux ongles des harpies,
Sauront jusqu'à son cœur se frayer un chemin.

Comme un tout jeune oiseau qui tremble et qui palpite,
J'arracherai ce cœur tout rouge de son sein,
Et, pour rassasier ma bête favorite,
Je le lui jetterai par terre avec dédain!"

He disports with the wind, holds converse with the clouds,
And feels rapture in chanting the Way of the Cross;
And the Spirit attending his journey through life
Is in tears to behold him as blithe as a bird.

All those he would love look upon him with fear,
Or else, waxing bold at his silence and calm,
Try to see who can cause him to cry out in pain,
And on him make the test of how cruel they can be.

The bread and the wine that are meant for his mouth
They sprinkle with ashes, with spittle befoul;
Whatever he touches they piously spurn,
And repent having stepped where his feet have once trod.

His woman proclaims to whoever will hear:
"Since my beauty so worthy of worship he finds,
Of antiquity's idols I'll play the old game,
And like them I shall have myself gilded anew;

And I'll revel in spikenard, in incense and myrrh,
In meek genuflections, in viands and wines,
Just to see if I can, in a heart that loves me,
Usurp, for a laugh, its devotion to God!

And when I grow tired of this impious farce,
I shall then lay upon him my frail, potent hand,
And my nails, like the harpies' redoubtable claws,
Will dig their way forcibly right to his heart.

That heart, like a fluttering, trembling young bird,
I shall tear out all crimson and raw from his breast,
And to gorge to repletion my precious pet dog,
I shall throw it disdainfully down on the ground!"

Vers le Ciel, où son œil voit un trône splendide,
Le Poëte serein lève ses bras pieux,
Et les vastes éclairs de son esprit lucide
Lui dérobent l'aspect des peuples furieux:

—"Soyez béni, mon Dieu, qui donnez la souffrance
Comme un divin remède à nos impuretés
Et comme la meilleure et la plus pure essence
Qui prépare les forts aux saintes voluptés!

Je sais que vous gardez une place au Poëte
Dans les rangs bienheureux des saintes Légions,
Et que vous l'invitez à l'éternelle fête
Des Trônes, des Vertus, des Dominations.

Je sais que la douleur est la noblesse unique
Où ne mordront jamais la terre et les enfers,
Et qu'il faut pour tresser ma couronne mystique
Imposer tous les temps et tous les univers.

Mais les bijoux perdus de l'antique Palmyre,
Les métaux inconnus, les perles de la mer,
Par votre main montés, ne pourraient pas suffire
A ce beau diadème éblouissant et clair;

Car il ne sera fait que de pure lumière,
Puisée au foyer saint des rayons primitifs,
Et dont les yeux mortels, dans leur splendeur entière,
Ne sont que des miroirs obscurcis et plaintifs!"

Toward Heaven, where his eye sees a glorious throne,
The Poet serene lifts his reverent arms,
And the far-flashing gleams of his spirit's clear flame
Make him blind to his fellow-man's furious glares:

—"Be blessèd, O God, you who suffering give
As a physic divine for our grossness and flaws,
And the purest and best of all essences rare,
Which readies the strong for beatified bliss!

I know that you keep for the Poet a place
In the thrice-blessed ranks of the Legions of Saints,
And eternal rejoicing invite him to share
With the choirs of the Virtues, Dominions and Thrones.

I know that affliction's the only noblesse
Which the earth and all Hades can never corrode,
And that weaving my mystical crown must impose
On all aeons of time and the whole universe.

But not all of ancient Palmyra's lost gems,
The rare precious metals, the pearls of the sea,
Enchased by your very own hand, would suffice
For that beautiful diadem dazzling and bright;

For it will be made of naught else but pure light
From the sacred fount dipped, from the source of prime rays,
And of which mortal eyes, in their splendor entire,
Are no more than mirrors, plaintive and bedimmed!"

Charles Baudelaire

L'Albatros

Souvent, pour s'amuser, les hommes d'équipage
Prennent des albatros, vastes oiseaux des mers,
Qui suivent, indolents compagnons de voyage,
Le navire glissant sur les gouffres amers.

A peine les ont-ils déposés sur les planches,
Que ces rois de l'azur, maladroits et honteux,
Laissent piteusement leurs grandes ailes blanches
Comme des avirons traîner à côté d'eux.

Ce voyageur ailé, comme il est gauche et veule!
Lui, naguère si beau, qu'il est comique et laid!
L'un agace son bec avec un brûle-gueule,
L'autre mime, en boitant, l'infirme qui volait!

Le Poëte est semblable au prince des nuées
Qui hante la tempête et se rit de l'archer;
Exilé sur le sol, au milieu des huées,
Ses ailes de géant l'empêchent de marcher.

The Albatross

Ofttimes, for amusement, the men of a crew
Will capture an albatross, one of those huge
Fellow-traveler sea-birds who indolently
Follow ships as they skim the salt deeps of the sea.

No sooner deposed on the planks of the deck
Than this king of the blue, maladroit and shamefaced,
Lets his great snow-white wings droop piteously,
Like cumbersome oars being dragged at his sides.

This tireless winged voyager—how clumsy and weak!
What's become of his beauty? He's ugly, absurd!
With a mug-scorcher* one sailor pokes at his beak;
Another mocks, limping, the cripple who soared!

The Poet resembles this prince of the clouds,
Who seeks out the storm and derides lightning-shafts;**
Exiled here on the ground, amid jeers at each fall,
His giant's wings keep him from walking at all.

* Mug-scorcher: a sailor's short-stemmed pipe, commonly
   called a "cutty-pipe."

** Lightning-shafts: the "arrows" of the storm-god. After all,
   what human *archer* would be wasting arrows, during a
   storm at sea?

Charles Baudelaire

Elévation

Au-dessus des étangs, au-dessus des vallées,
Des montagnes, des bois, des nuages, des mers,
Par delà le soleil, par delà les éthers,
Par delà les confins des sphères étoilées,

Mon esprit, tu te meus avec agilité,
Et, comme un bon nageur qui se pâme dans l'onde,
Tu sillonnes gaiement l'immensité profonde
Avec une indicible et mâle volupté.

Envole-toi bien loin de ces miasmes morbides;
Va te purifier dans l'air supérieur,
Et bois, comme une pure et divine liqueur,
Le feu clair qui remplit les espaces limpides.

Derrière les ennuis et les vastes chagrins
Qui chargent de leur poids l'existence brumeuse,
Heureux celui qui peut d'une aile vigoureuse
S'élancer vers les champs lumineux et sereins;

Celui dont les pensers, comme des alouettes,
Vers les cieux le matin prennent un libre essor,
—Qui plane sur la vie, et comprend sans effort
Le langage des fleurs et des choses muettes!

Elevation

Above ponds and lakes, above valleys and dales,
Above mountains and forests and clouds and the seas,
Past the sun, to ethereal space and beyond,
Beyond the confines of the star-spangled spheres,

My spirit, you move with alacritous ease,
And like a good swimmer who basks in the wave,
You delightedly furrow the infinite deep
With a virile, ineffably sensual joy.

From these morbid miasmas fly far, far away;
Go and make yourself pure in the high upper air,
And imbibe, like an untainted nectar divine,
The bright glow that pervades the clear reaches of space.

From behind the great mass of afflictions and woes
That encumber this earthly existence opaque,
Most fortunate he who on powerful wings
Can soar upward to meadows of luminous calm;

He whose thoughts in the morning, like midsummer larks,
In freedom take flight to the heavens above,
—Who can float above life, and with ease comprehend
The language of flowers and of all voiceless things!

Correspondances

La Nature est un temple où de vivants piliers
Laissent parfois sortir de confuses paroles;
L'homme y passe à travers des forêts de symboles
Qui l'observent avec des regards familiers.

Comme de longs échos qui de loin se confondent
Dans une ténébreuse et profonde unité,
Vaste comme la nuit et comme la clarté,
Les parfums, les couleurs et les sons se répondent.

Il est des parfums frais comme des chairs d'enfants,
Doux comme les hautbois, verts comme les prairies,
—Et d'autres, corrompus, riches et triomphants,

Ayant l'expansion des choses infinies,
Comme l'ambre, le musc, le benjoin et l'encens
Qui chantent les transports de l'esprit et des sens.

Charles Baudelaire

Correspondences

All Nature's a temple whose pillars, alive,
Sometimes utter words indistinct and unclear;
Man passes through forests of symbols therein
Which observe him with knowing, familiar regards.

Like lingering echoes that blend from afar
Into incomprehensible oneness profound,
Immense as the night and the clear light of day,
Certain fragrances, colors and sounds correspond.

There are scents fresh and cool like the flesh of a child,
Clear and dulcet like oboes, soft green like the fields,
—And others, corrupt, overpowering and rich,

That have the expansion of infinite things,
Such as ambergris, benjamin, musk and incense,
Which sing of the transports of spirit and sense.

Les Phares

Rubens, fleuve d'oubli, jardin de la paresse,
Oreiller de chair fraîche où l'on ne peut aimer,
Mais où la vie afflue et s'agite sans cesse,
Comme l'air dans le ciel et la mer dans la mer;

Léonard de Vinci, miroir profond et sombre,
Où des anges charmants, avec un doux souris
Tout chargé de mystère, apparaissent à l'ombre
Des glaciers et des pins qui ferment leur pays;

Rembrandt, triste hôpital tout rempli de murmures,
Et d'un grand crucifix décoré seulement,
Où la prière en pleurs s'exhale des ordures,
Et d'un rayon d'hiver traversé brusquement;

Michel-Ange, lieu vague où l'on voit des Hercules
Se mêler à des Christs, et se lever tout droits
Des fantômes puissants qui dans des crépuscules
Déchirent leur suaire en étirant leurs doigts;

Colères de boxeur, impudences de faune,
Toi qui sus ramasser la beauté des goujats,
Grand cœur gonflé d'orgueil, homme débile et jaune,
Puget, mélancolique empereur des forçats;

Watteau, ce carnaval où bien des cœurs illustres,
Comme des papillons, errent en flamboyant,
Décors frais et légers éclairés par des lustres
Qui versent la folie à ce bal tournoyant;

The Beacons

Rubens, Lethe's river, lazy garden of ease,
Freshened pillow of flesh where one cannot make love
But where life teems and surges and ceaselessly stirs,
Like the winds in the air and the tides in the sea;

Leonardo da Vinci, dark mirror and deep,
Where angels enchanting, with sweet gentle smiles
Enigmatic, appear against backgrounds composed
Of the snow-fields and pines which their homeland enclose;

Rembrandt, sad hospital filled with soft moans
And by one great crucifix solely adorned,
Where prayer is exhaled from the refuse in tears,
And brusquely traversed by a wintry sun's ray;

Michelangelo, limbo where muscular Greeks
Intermingle with Christs, and where powerful ghosts
Are seen rising up straight in a murky half-light
And with tense, straining fingers, tearing their shrouds;

A prize-fighter's anger, a faun's impudence,
You who knew how to capture the beauty of churls,
Great pride-swollen heart in a weak, jaundiced man,
Puget, gloomy emperor of convicts in chains;

Watteau, carnival where illustrious souls
In great number like flamboyant butterflies flit,
Light and airy decors lit by great chandeliers,
Which shed a mad glow on this whirling dress-ball;

Goya, cauchemar plein de choses inconnues,
De fœtus qu'on fait cuire au milieu des sabbats,
De vieilles au miroir et d'enfants toutes nues,
Pour tenter les démons ajustant bien leurs bas;

Delacroix, lac de sang hanté des mauvais anges,
Ombragé par un bois de sapins toujours vert,
Où, sous un ciel chagrin, des fanfares étranges
Passent, comme un soupir étouffé de Weber;

Ces malédictions, ces blasphèmes, ces plaintes,
Ces extases, ces cris, ces pleurs, ces *Te Deum*,
Sont un écho redit par mille labyrinthes;
C'est pour les cœurs mortels un divin opium!

C'est un cri répété par mille sentinelles,
Un ordre renvoyé par mille porte-voix;
C'est un phare allumé sur mille citadelles,
Un appel de chasseurs perdus dans les grands bois!

Car c'est vraiment, Seigneur, le meilleur témoignage
Que nous puissions donner de notre dignité
Que cet ardent sanglot qui roule d'âge en âge
Et vient mourir au bord de votre éternité!

Goya, eerie nightmare of things never known,
Of fœtuses cooking in witch-sabbath pots,
Of hags at the mirror and nude little girls
Adjusting their stockings the demons to tempt;

Delacroix, lake of blood where the bad angels throng,
Set within a dark forest of evergreen pines,
Where beneath a bleak sky, strange and wondrous brass bands
Pass along, like a muffled, suppressed Weber sigh;

These curses, these blasphemies, wailings and moans,
These ecstasies, outcries, *Te Deum*'s and tears,
Are a thousandfold echo from labyrinth walls;
For all mortal hearts, it's an opium divine!

It's a password repeated by thousands of guards,
An order through thousands of megaphones barked;
It's a beacon on thousands of citadels fired,
A distress call from hunters lost deep in the woods!

For it's truly, O Lord, the best evidence
We could possibly give of our worth here on earth—
This great ardent sob which from age rolls to age
And at last comes to Thee, on eternity's shore!

Charles Baudelaire

Le Mauvais Moine

Les cloîtres anciens sur leurs grandes murailles
Etalaient en tableaux la sainte Vérité,
Dont l'effet, réchauffant les pieuses entrailles,
Tempérait la froideur de leur austérité.

En ces temps où du Christ florissaient les semailles,
Plus d'un illustre moine, aujourd'hui peu cité,
Prenant pour atelier le champ des funérailles,
Glorifiait la Mort avec simplicité.

—Mon âme est un tombeau que, mauvais cénobite,
Depuis l'éternité je parcours et j'habite;
Rien n'embellit les murs de ce cloître odieux.

O moine fainéant! quand saurai-je donc faire
Du spectacle vivant de ma triste misère
Le travail de mes mains et l'amour de mes yeux?

Charles Baudelaire

The Bad Monk

Monasteries of old, on their great inner walls,
Used to show forth in paintings the scriptural Truth,
Which by warming the pious insides of the monks
Served to temper the cold of their austerity.

In those times when the seeds of the Christ grew apace,
More than one worthy monk, little noted today,
Taking burial-grounds for his workshop in stone,
Used to celebrate Death with devout naïveté.

—My soul is a tomb which, a bad cenobite,
I have trodden and dwelt in since time first began;
Yet the walls of this odious cloister are bare.

Idle monk that I am! When then shall I learn
To make of my wretchedness' live horror-show
The work of my hands and the love of my eyes?

L'Ennemi

Ma jeunesse ne fut qu'un ténébreux orage,
Traversé çà et là par de brillants soleils;
Le tonnerre et la pluie ont fait un tel ravage,
Qu'il reste en mon jardin bien peu de fruits vermeils.

Voilà que j'ai touché l'automne des idées,
Et qu'il faut employer la pelle et les râteaux
Pour rassembler à neuf les terres inondées,
Où l'eau creuse des trous grands comme des tombeaux.

Et qui sait si les fleurs nouvelles que je rêve
Trouveront dans ce sol lavé comme une grève
Le mystique aliment qui ferait leur vigueur?

—O douleur! ô douleur! Le Temps mange la vie,
Et l'obscur Ennemi qui nous ronge le cœur
Du sang que nous perdons croît et se fortifie!

The Foe

My youth was naught else but a dark, raging storm,
Traversed here and there by a ray of bright sun;
The thunder and rain wrought such havoc and harm
That but few crimson fruits in my garden remain.

Now it seems I have reached the autumn of ideas,
And must use in that garden the spade and the rake
To make whole once again the inundated ground,
Where the water has hollowed out holes big as graves.

And who knows if the new blooms I'm now dreaming of
Will find in this soil, washed and leached like a strand,
The mystical food which would cause them to thrive?

O sorrow! O grief! Life is eaten by Time,
And the dark, deadly Foe who still gnaws at our hearts,
From the blood that we lose, grows gigantic and strong!

Le Guignon

Pour soulever un poids si lourd,
Sisyphe, il faudrait ton courage!
Bien qu'on ait du cœur à l'ouvrage,
L'Art est long et le Temps est court.

Loin des sépultures célèbres,
Vers un cimetière isolé,
Mon cœur, comme un tambour voilé,
Va battant des marches funèbres.

—Maint joyau dort enseveli
Dans les ténèbres et l'oubli,
Bien loin des pioches et des sondes;

Mainte fleur épanche à regret
Son parfum doux comme un secret
Dans les solitudes profondes.

Ill-Starred

To lift and bear so great a weight
Would take thy courage, Sisyphus!
Although one's heart be in the task,
Art is long and Time is short.

Far from glory's sepulchers,
Toward some burial-ground remote,
My heart now, like a muffled drum,
Is beating out a funeral march.

Many a jewel buried sleeps
In darkness and oblivion,
Beyond the reach of pick or plumb;

Many a flower, regretfully,
Wafts forth its secret-sweet perfume
In lonely deserts vast and deep.

La Vie antérieure

J'ai longtemps habité sous de vastes portiques
Que les soleils marins teignaient de mille feux,
Et que leurs grands piliers, droits et majestueux,
Rendaient pareils, le soir, aux grottes basaltiques.

Les houles, en roulant les images des cieux,
Mêlaient d'une façon solennelle et mystique
Les tout-puissants accords de leur riche musique
Aux couleurs du couchant reflété par mes yeux.

C'est là que j'ai vécu dans les voluptés calmes,
Au milieu de l'azur, des vagues, des splendeurs
Et des esclaves nus, tout imprégnés d'odeurs,

Qui me rafraîchissaient le front avec des palmes,
Et dont l'unique soin était d'approfondir
Le secret douloureux qui me faisait languir.

Charles Baudelaire

The Previous Life

For a long time I dwelt beneath vast porticoes
That the sun and the sea tinged with myriad fires,
And whose columns majestic, so straight and so tall,
Made them look like, at evening, basaltic grottoes.

The long swells, reflecting the skies as they rolled,
Would blend, in a solemn and mystical way,
The all-powerful chords of their music so rich
With the hues of the sunset my eyes mirrored there.

It was there that I lived in voluptuous calm,
Amid blue skies, and waves, and rich splendors galore,
And attended by highly-perfumed naked slaves,

Who would cool my brow for me with fronds of the palm,
And whose one great concern was to try to divine
The dolorous secret that caused me to pine.

Bohémiens en voyage

La tribu prophétique aux prunelles ardentes
Hier s'est mise en route, emportant ses petits
Sur son dos, ou livrant à leurs fiers appétits
Le trésor toujours prêt des mamelles pendantes.

Les hommes vont à pied sous leurs armes luisantes
Le long des chariots où les leurs sont blottis,
Promenant sur le ciel des yeux appesantis
Par le morne regret des chimères absentes.

Du fond de son réduit sablonneux, le grillon,
Les regardant passer, redouble sa chanson;
Cybèle, qui les aime, augmente ses verdures,

Fait couler le rocher et fleurir le désert
Devant ces voyageurs, pour lesquels est ouvert
L'empire familier des ténèbres futures.

Charles Baudelaire

Gypsies on the Move

The prophetical tribe with the burning dark eyes
Took the road yesterday with their babes pickaback,
Or regaling their fine hearty appetites with
The convenient treasure of pendulous breasts.

Bearing weapons agleam, the men stride alongside
The wagons that shelter the ones they hold dear,
Ever scanning the skies with eyes heavy and sad,
As if mourning the absence of visions now fled.

The cricket, from deep in his sandy redoubt,
As he watches their passing, redoubles his song;
Cybele, who loves them, her verdure augments,

Makes the rock to gush water, the desert to bloom
For these wanderers with access, familiar and free,
To the future's obscure and inscrutable realm.

Charles Baudelaire

L'Homme et la Mer

Homme libre, toujours tu chériras la mer!
La mer est ton miroir; tu contemples ton âme
Dans le déroulement infini de sa lame,
Et ton esprit n'est pas un gouffre moins amer.

Tu te plais à plonger au sein de ton image;
Tu l'embrasses des yeux et des bras, et ton cœur
Se distrait quelquefois de sa propre rumeur
Au bruit de cette plainte indomptable et sauvage.

Vous êtes tous les deux ténébreux et discrets:
Homme, nul n'a sondé le fond de tes abîmes,
O mer, nul ne connaît tes richesses intimes,
Tant vous êtes jaloux de garder vos secrets.

Et cependant voilà des siècles innombrables
Que vous vous combattiez sans pitié ni remord,
Tellement vous aimez le carnage et la mort,
O lutteurs éternels, ô frères implacables!

Man and the Sea

Free man, you forever will cherish the sea!
The sea is your mirror; you ▓▓▓▓ your own soul   *perceive*
In the infinite rolling and sweep of her wave,
And your mind is a gulf no less bitter and deep.

You enjoy plunging into your counterpart's breast;
You embrace her with eyes and with arms, and your heart
Is distracted at times from its own pounding beat
By the sound of that murmur so fierce and untamed.

Both of you are mysterious, secretive, discreet;
O man, none has fathomed the depths you can sink to;
O sea, no one knows what rich treasures you hold,
So jealous you are, your dark secrets to keep.

And yet for numberless centuries past
You have fought one another sans pity or qualm,
So much do you love dealing carnage and death,
O eternal combatants, implacable twins!

La Beauté

Je suis belle, ô mortels! comme un rêve de pierre,
Et mon sein, où chacun s'est meurtri tour à tour,
Est fait pour inspirer au poète un amour
Eternel et muet ainsi que la matière.

Je trône dans l'azur comme un sphinx incompris;
J'unis un cœur de neige à la blancheur des cygnes;
Je hais le mouvement qui déplace les lignes,
Et jamais je ne pleure et jamais je ne ris.

Les poètes, devant mes grandes attitudes,
Que j'ai l'air d'emprunter aux plus fiers monuments,
Consumeront leurs jours en d'austères études;

Car j'ai, pour fasciner ces dociles amants,
De purs miroirs qui font toutes choses plus belles:
Mes yeux, mes larges yeux aux clartés éternelles!

Beauty

I'm beautiful, O mortals! like a dream in stone,
And my breast, where each one has been bruised in his turn,
Is fashioned to inspire the poet with a love
As mute and as eternal as the stone itself.

I sit in azure state, like an unfathomed sphinx;
I join a heart of snow to swans' unsullied white;
I abhor movement, which displaces lovely lines,
And never do I laugh and never do I weep.

Poets, confronted by my striking attitudes,
Which I seem to borrow from proudest monuments,
Will waste their lives in solemn study of me; for

I have, with which to charm these docile paramours,
Pure mirrors rendering all things more beautiful:
My eyes, my two wide eyes with lights forever bright!

La Géante

Du temps que la Nature en sa verve puissante
Concevait chaque jour des enfants monstrueux,
J'eusse aimé vivre auprès d'une jeune géante,
Comme aux pieds d'une reine un chat voluptueux.

J'eusse aimé voir son corps fleurir avec son âme
Et grandir librement dans ses terribles jeux;
Deviner si son cœur couve une sombre flamme
Aux humides brouillards qui nagent dans ses yeux;

Parcourir à loisir ses magnifiques formes;
Ramper sur le versant de ses genoux énormes,
Et parfois en été, quand les soleils malsains,

Lasse, la font s'étendre à travers la campagne,
Dormir nonchalamment à l'ombre de ses seins,
Comme un hameau paisible au pied d'une montagne.

The Giantess

In the time when Nature, in her power and zest,
Used to conceive each day some sort of monster-child,
I would have liked to live with a young giantess,
Like a voluptuous cat at the feet of a queen.

I would have liked to see her bloom, body and soul,
And grow up freely playing her prodigious games;
To guess if some dark flame was smouldering in her heart
By watching the damp mists that floated in her eyes;

To roam at will upon her parts magnificent,
To clamber up and down in her enormous lap,
And sometimes in summer when, tired by baneful sun,

She stretched out at full length across the countryside,
To sleep insouciant in her great bosoms' shade,
Like a peaceful hamlet at a mountain's foot.

Parfum exotique

Quand, les deux yeux fermés, en un soir chaud d'automne,
Je respire l'odeur de ton sein chaleureux,
Je vois se dérouler des rivages heureux
Qu'éblouissent les feux d'un soleil monotone;

Une île paresseuse où la nature donne
Des arbres singuliers et des fruits savoureux;
Des hommes dont le corps est mince et vigoureux,
Et des femmes dont l'œil par sa franchise étonne.

Guidé par ton odeur vers de charmants climats,
Je vois un port rempli de voiles et de mâts
Encor tout fatigués par la vague marine,

Pendant que le parfum des verts tamariniers,
Qui circule dans l'air et m'enfle la narine,
Se mêle dans mon âme au chant des mariniers.

Exotic Perfume

perfume

When with my two eyes closed, on a warm autumn eve,
I breathe the odor of your bosom warm and sweet,
I see unfold a vision of a blissful shore
Ashimmer in the blaze of an unfailing sun;

A lazy, languid isle where Nature lavishes
A wealth of curious trees and savory strange fruits;
Where live strong-bodied men, slim, lithe and vigorous,
And women who surprise by the candor of their eyes.

Led by your odor to delightful distant climes,
I see a busy harbor filled with sails and masts
Still weary from their struggles with the ocean wave,

While the exotic scent of green tamarind trees,
Which hovers in the air and makes my nostrils flare,
Is blended in my soul with chants of mariners.

De profundis clamavi

J'implore ta pitié, Toi, l'unique que j'aime,
Du fond du gouffre obscur où mon cœur est tombé.
C'est un univers morne à l'horizon plombé,
Où nagent dans la nuit l'horreur et le blasphème.

Un soleil sans chaleur plane au-dessus six mois,
Et les six autres mois la nuit couvre la terre;
C'est un pays plus nu que la terre polaire;
—Ni bêtes, ni ruisseaux, ni verdure, ni bois!

Or il n'est pas d'horreur au monde qui surpasse
La froide cruauté de ce soleil de glace
Et cette immense nuit semblable au vieux Chaos;

Je jalouse le sort des plus vils animaux
Qui peuvent se plonger dans un sommeil stupide,
Tant l'écheveau du temps lentement se dévide!

De profundis clamavi

I beg for thy pity, O Thou,* my only love,
From the deep, dark abyss where my heart lies entombed.
It's a bleak, dismal world of horizons lead-gray,
Where horror and blasphemy swirl in the gloom.

A sun without warmth hangs above for six months,
And the other six months darkness blankets the land;
It's a country more stark than the earth at the poles:
—No greenery, no forests, no creatures, no streams!

Now no horror in all the wide world can surpass
The cold, cruel glare of this sun made of ice
And this measureless night like the Chaos of old;

I envy the lot of the meanest of beasts
Who can plunge themselves into the stupor of sleep,
So slowly unravels the long skein of time!

* God,

Harmonie du soir

Voici venir les temps où vibrant sur sa tige
Chaque fleur s'évapore ainsi qu'un encensoir;
Les sons et les parfums tournent dans l'air du soir;
Valse mélancolique et langoureux vertige!

Chaque fleur s'évapore ainsi qu'un encensoir;
Le violon frémit comme un cœur qu'on afflige;
Valse mélancolique et langoureux vertige!
Le ciel est triste et beau comme un grand reposoir.

Le violon frémit comme un cœur qu'on afflige,
Un cœur tendre, qui hait le néant vaste et noir!
Le ciel est triste et beau comme un grand reposoir;
Le soleil s'est noyé dans son sang qui se fige.

Un cœur tendre, qui hait le néant vaste et noir,
Du passé lumineux recueille tout vestige!
Le soleil s'est noyé dans son sang qui se fige . . .
Ton souvenir en moi luit comme un ostensoir!

Evening Harmony

And now the time has come when, trembling on its stem,
Each flower, like a censer, into scent dissolves;
Then sounds and perfumes mingle in the evening air;
A melancholy waltz, a languid vertigo!

Each flower, like a censer, into scent dissolves;
The violin laments like an afflicted heart;
A melancholy waltz, a languid vertigo!
The sky is sad and lovely like a *reposoir*.*

The violin laments like an afflicted heart,
A tender heart, which hates the vast dark nothingness!
The sky is sad and lovely like a *reposoir*.*
The sun has drowned itself in its congealing blood.

A tender heart, which hates the vast dark nothingness,
Will cherish every vestige of the glowing past!
The sun has drowned itself in its congealing blood . . .
Your memory shines within me like an *ostensoir*.**

* *reposoir*:   a station or temporary altar, when the Host is
             carried in procession.

**ostensoir*:   a golden receptacle in which the Host is held.

Le Flacon

Il est de forts parfums pour qui toute matière
Est poreuse. On dirait qu'ils pénètrent le verre.
En ouvrant un coffret venu de l'Orient
Dont la serrure grince et rechigne en criant,

Ou dans une maison déserte quelque armoire
Pleine de l'âcre odeur des temps, poudreuse et noire,
Parfois on trouve un vieux flacon qui se souvient,
D'où jaillit toute vive une âme qui revient.

Mille pensers dormaient, chrysalides funèbres,
Frémissant doucement dans les lourdes ténèbres,
Qui dégagent leur aile et prennent leur essor,
Teintés d'azur, glacés de rose, lamés d'or.

Voilà le souvenir enivrant qui voltige
Dans l'air troublé; les yeux se ferment; le Vertige
Saisit l'âme vaincue et la pousse à deux mains
Vers un gouffre obscurci de miasmes humains;

Il la terrasse au bord d'un gouffre séculaire,
Où, Lazare odorant déchirant son suaire,
Se meut dans son réveil le cadavre spectral
D'un vieil amour ranci, charmant et sépulcral.

Ainsi, quand je serai perdu dans la mémoire
Des hommes, dans le coin d'une sinistre armoire
Quand on m'aura jeté, vieux flacon désolé,
Décrépit, poudreux, sale, abject, visqueux, fêlé,

The Phial

Transmigrate through glass.

For some potent perfumes, any substance at all
Is porous. It's as if they ~~pass right through the glass.~~
Upon opening a chest from the far Orient,
Whose hinges and lock creak and groan in protest,

Or some ancient armoire in a vacated house,
Full of time's acrid mustiness, dusty and dark,
One may find an old phial that remembers the past,
Whence emerges, alive, a returning soul's ghost.

Dormant thoughts by the thousand, forlorn chrysalids,
Softly quivering there in the close, humid dark,
Unfold and deploy their sheer wings and take flight,
Tinted azure, glazed roseate, spangled with gold.

Then it's heady remembrance that flutters about
In the unquiet air; the eyes close; Vertigo
Grips the overborne soul and impels with both hands
Toward a chasm by human miasmas obscured;

Knocks it down at the brink of a secular gulf,
Where, a sweet-smelling Lazarus tearing his shroud,
There awakens and stirs the cadaverous ghost
Of an old love turned rancid, sepulchral and suave.

So, when I have been lost in the memory of men,
When off into a corner of some foul armoire
They have cast me, a sorry, decrepit old phial,
Thick with dust, filthy, slimy, repulsive and cracked,

Je serai ton cercueil, aimable pestilence!
Le témoin de ta force et de ta virulence,
Cher poison préparé par les anges! liqueur
Qui me ronge, ô la vie et la mort de mon cœur!

I shall then be thy coffin, beloved pestilence!
The proof of thy potency and virulence,
Thou dear poison prepared by the angels! Liqueur
That destroys me, O life of my heart and its death!

Charles Baudelaire

L'Invitation au voyage

Mon enfant, ma soeur,
Songe à la douceur
D'aller là-bas vivre ensemble!
Aimer à loisir,
Aimer et mourir
Au pays qui te ressemble!
Les soleils mouillés
De ces ciels brouillés
Pour mon esprit ont les charmes
Si mystérieux
De tes traîtres yeux,
Brillant à travers leurs larmes.

Là, tout n'est qu'ordre et beauté,
Luxe, calme et volupté.

Des meubles luisants,
Polis par les ans,
Décoreraient notre chambre;
Les plus rares fleurs
Mêlant leurs odeurs
Aux vagues senteurs de l'ambre,
Les riches plafonds,
Les miroirs profonds,
La splendeur orientale,
Tout y parlerait
A l'âme en secret
Sa douce langue natale.

Invitation to the Voyage

Darling, sister mine,
Think how sweet 'twould be
To go live together there!
To love at our ease,
To live, love and die
In that land so like yourself!
The suns blurred by rain
In those cloudy skies
For my spirit have the charms
So mysterious
Of your traitress eyes,
Through their tears shining brightly.

There, all is order, beauty,
Luxury, pleasure and calm.

Gleaming chests and chairs,
Burnished by the years,
Would decorate our chamber;
Rarest flowers in bloom
Blending their perfume
With the faint scent of amber,
Ceilings rich, deep-banked
Mirrors to reflect
Oriental pomp and splendor,
All things there would speak
To the secret soul
In their soft native language.

Là, tout n'est qu'ordre et beauté,
Luxe, calme et volupté.

Vois sur ces canaux
    Dormir ces vaisseaux
Dont l'humeur est vagabonde;
    C'est pour assouvir
    Ton moindre désir
Qu'ils viennent du bout du monde.
    —Les soleils couchants
    Revêtent les champs,
Les canaux, la ville entière,
    D'hyacinthe et d'or;
    Le monde s'endort
Dans une chaude lumière.

Là, tout n'est qu'ordre et beauté,
Luxe, calme et volupté.

There, all is order, beauty,
Luxury, pleasure and calm.

See on yon canals,
    Sleeping now, those ships
Whose mood is vagabonding.
    'Tis to gratify
    Your slightest desire
That they've come from distant climes.
    —Now the setting sun
    Is clothing the fields
The canals, the town entire,
    In jacinth and gold;
    The world's being lulled
To sleep in a warming light.

There, all is order, beauty,
Luxury, pleasure and calm.

Chant d'automne

I

Bientôt nous plongerons dans les froides ténèbres;
Adieu, vive clarté de nos étés trop courts!
J'entends déjà tomber avec des chocs funèbres
Le bois retentissant sur le pavé des cours.

Tout l'hiver va rentrer dans mon être: colère,
Haine, frissons, horreur, labeur dur et forcé,
Et, comme le soleil dans son enfer polaire,
Mon cœur ne sera plus qu'un bloc rouge et glacé.

J'écoute en frémissant chaque bûche qui tombe;
L'échafaud qu'on bâtit n'a pas d'écho plus sourd.
Mon esprit est pareil à la tour qui succombe
Sous les coups du bélier infatigable et lourd.

Il me semble, bercé par ce choc monotone,
Qu'on cloue en grande hâte un cercueil quelque part . . .
Pour qui? —C'était hier l'été; voici l'automne!
Ce bruit mystérieux sonne comme un départ.

II

J'aime de vos longs yeux la lumière verdâtre,
Douce beauté, mais tout aujourd'hui m'est amer,
Et rien, ni votre amour, ni le boudoir, ni l'âtre,
Ne me vaut le soleil rayonnant sur la mer.

Et pourtant aimez-moi, tendre cœur! soyez mère
Même pour un ingrat, même pour un méchant;

Charles Baudelaire

Autumn Song

I

Very soon we'll be plunged into cold, gloomy dark;
O clear light of all-too-brief summer, farewell!
Already I hear the lugubrious thump
Of wood being dropped on courtyard paving-stones.

Once again, all of winter will enter my being:
Anger, hate, disgust, shudders; forced, joyless toil;
And my heart, like the sun in its great polar hell,
Will be naught any more but a frozen red lump.

I listen, and quake at the fall of each log;
No gibbet a-building has an echo more grim;
My spirit succumbs, as the tower to the blows
Of the ponderous, tireless battering-ram.

As I'm lulled by this monotone thudding, it seems
That they're hastily nailing a coffin somewhere . . .
For whom? —In one day, summer's gone, and it's fall!
This strange sound has the ring of a funeral knell.

II

I love the greenish glint of your almond-long eyes,
Beauty sweet, but today for me all is gall,
And no thing—not your love, the boudoir, nor the hearth,
Is to me worth the sun beaming down on the sea.

Yet love me, tender heart! Be what a mother is
To even a thankless, even a wicked son;

Amante ou soeur, soyez la douceur éphémère
D'un glorieux automne ou d'un soleil couchant.

Courte tache! La tombe attend; elle est avide!
Ah! laissez-moi, mon front posé sur vos genoux,
Goûter, en regrettant l'été blanc et torride,
De l'arrière-saison le rayon jaune et doux!

Lover or sister, be the transitory bliss
Of a glorious autumn or a setting sun.

Brief task! for the grave, ever eager, awaits!
So let me, lying here with my head in your lap,
Regretting the torrid white summer, enjoy
The soft golden glow of late autumn's last days!

Charles Baudelaire

A une dame créole

Au pays parfumé que le soleil caresse,
J'ai connu, sous un dais d'arbres tout empourprés
Et de palmiers d'où pleut sur les yeux la paresse,
Une dame créole aux charmes ignorés.

Son teint est pâle et chaud; la brune enchanteresse
A dans le cou des airs noblement maniérés;
Grande et svelte en marchant comme une chasseresse,
Son sourire est tranquille et ses yeux assurés.

Si vous alliez, Madame, au vrai pays de gloire,
Sur les bords de la Seine ou de la verte Loire,
Belle digne d'orner les antiques manoirs,

Vous feriez, à l'abri des ombreuses retraites,
Germer mille sonnets dans le cœur des poëtes,
Que vos grands yeux rendraient plus soumis que vos noirs.

Charles Baudelaire

To a Creole Lady

In a spice-scented country caressed by the sun,
'Neath an awning of trees all empurpled with bloom
And of palms dripping sloth on the eyes, I once met
A fine Creole lady of singular charms.

Her fair skin's warm of tone; the enchantress brunette
Bears her head with a mannered air, noble and proud;
Tall and svelte, with the stride of a huntress she moves;
Her smile is serene and her glance self-assured.

Should you travel, Milady, to glory's true home
On the banks of the Seine or the emerald Loire,
O beauty to grace any ancient *manoir*,

You would cause, in the shelter of shady retreats,
Many sonnets to sprout in the hearts of our bards,
Whom your great eyes would leave more enslaved
                             than your blacks.

Tristesses de la lune

Ce soir, la lune rêve avec plus de paresse;
Ainsi qu'une beauté, sur de nombreux coussins,
Qui d'une main distraite et légère caresse
Avant de s'endormir le contour de ses seins,

Sur le dos satiné des molles avalanches,
Mourante, elle se livre aux longues pâmoisons,
Et promène ses yeux sur les visions blanches
Qui montent dans l'azur comme des floraisons.

Quand parfois sur ce globe, en sa langueur oisive,
Elle laisse filer une larme furtive,
Un poëte pieux, ennemi du sommeil,

Dans le creux de sa main prend cette larme pâle,
Aux reflets irisés comme un fragment d'opale,
Et la met dans son cœur loin des yeux du soleil.

Moon-Tears

The moon is most languidly dreaming tonight;
Like a beauty reclining on cushions galore
Who absently, lightly, ere falling asleep,
Caresses the curving contour of her breasts,

Aswoon on the satiny backs of that soft
Avalanche, into somnolent reverie she drifts,
And her eye wanders over the visions of white
Which like clusters of flowers rise into the night.

When sometimes, in her languorous spell, she lets fall
Onto this globe of ours a fugitive tear,
Some poet devout, adversary to sleep,

Will catch in the cup of his hand that pale tear,
Rainbow-hued like a fragment of opal, and hide
It away in his heart from the eye of the sun.

Charles Baudelaire

Les Chats

Les amoureux fervents et les savants austères
Aiment également, dans leur mûre saison,
Les chats puissants et doux, orgueil de la maison,
Qui comme eux sont frileux et comme eux sédentaires.

Amis de la science et de la volupté,
Ils cherchent le silence et l'horreur des ténèbres;
L'Erèbe les eût pris pour ses coursiers funèbres,
S'ils pouvaient au servage incliner leur fierté.

Ils prennent en songeant les nobles attitudes
Des grands sphinx allongés au fond des solitudes,
Qui semblent s'endormir dans un rêve sans fin;

Leurs reins féconds sont pleins d'étincelles magiques,
Et des parcelles d'or, ainsi qu'un sable fin,
Etoilent vaguement leurs prunelles mystiques.

Cats

Devout, fervent lovers and scholars austere,
In their ripe season, are equally fond
Of cats, sleek and powerful, pride of the house,
Who like them shun the cold and like them stay at home.

Well-disposed toward knowledge and pleasure, cats
Will seek out the silence and dread of the dark;
Great Erebus' funeral coursers they'd be,
Could they bend their proud spirit to servitude.

They assume, in their musing, the stately pose
Of great sphinxes reclining in vast lonely wastes,
Who seemingly drowse in a dream without end;

Full of magical sparks are their fecund loins,
And flecks of gold, like a fine-sprinkled sand,
Faintly bespangle their fathomless eyes.

Les Hiboux

Sous les ifs noirs qui les abritent,
Les hiboux se tiennent rangés,
Ainsi que des dieux étrangers,
Dardant leur œil rouge. Ils méditent.

Sans remuer ils se tiendront
Jusqu'à l'heure mélancolique
Où, poussant le soleil oblique,
Les ténèbres s'établiront.

Leur attitude au sage enseigne
Qu'il faut en ce monde qu'il craigne
Le tumulte et le mouvement;

L'homme ivre d'une ombre qui passe
Porte toujours le châtiment
D'avoir voulu changer de place.

Owls

In the black yews that shelter them,
The owls sit solemn and sedate,
Like alien gods, glaring about
With great red eyes. They meditate.

Quite motionless they will remain
Until the melancholy hour
When, pushing out the slanting sun,
Darkness everywhere will reign.

Their attitude instructs the wise
That in this world one must beware
Of movement, tumult and fanfare;

Whoso will passing shadows chase
The punishment must always bear
For having sought to change his place.

Sépulture

Si par une nuit lourde et sombre
Un bon chrétien, par charité,
Derrière quelque vieux décombre
Enterre votre corps vanté,

A l'heure où les chastes étoiles
Ferment leurs yeux appesantis,
L'araignée y fera ses toiles,
Et la vipère ses petits;

Vous entendrez toute l'année
Sur votre tête condamnée
Les cris lamentables des loups

Et des sorcières faméliques,
Les ébats des vieillards lubriques
Et les complots des noirs filous.

Interment

If on a dark and sultry night
Some good Samaritan inters
Behind some crumbling rubble-heap
That vaunted flesh-and-bone of yours,

When the chaste stars drowsy grow
And close their heavy-lidded eyes,
The spider there will spin her webs
And vipers will beget their young;

Throughout the year you'll surely hear
Above your poor, accursèd head
The lamentable howls of wolves

And shrieks of starveling witches dire,
The sport of lecherous old men
And the foul plots of evil rogues.

Charles Baudelaire

Une Gravure fantastique

Ce spectre singulier n'a pour toute toilette,
Grotesquement campé sur son front de squelette,
Qu'un diadème affreux sentant le carnaval.
Sans éperons, sans fouet, il essouffle un cheval,
Fantôme comme lui, rosse apocalyptique,
Qui bave des naseaux comme un épileptique.
Au travers de l'espace ils s'enfoncent tous deux,
Et foulent l'infini d'un sabot hasardeux.
Le cavalier promène un sabre qui flamboie
Sur les foules sans nom que sa monture broie,
Et parcourt, comme un prince inspectant sa maison,
Le cimetière immense et froid, sans horizon,
Où gisent, aux lueurs d'un soleil blanc et terne,
Les peuples de l'histoire ancienne et moderne.

A Fanciful Engraving

This singular specter for sole raiment wears,
Grotesquely clapped onto his skeleton brow,
A ghastly crown smacking of carnival show.
Without whip or spurs, he is winding a horse,
A phantom like him, a nag apocalyptic,
With nostrils afoam like an epileptic.
Through space they go plunging, the two as if one,
And trampling the infinite, reckless of hoof.
The rider is shaking a great flaming sword
At the nameless hosts whom his mount's riding down,
And inspecting on tour, like a prince his domain,
The immense cold necropolis, without horizon,
Where lie dead, in the light of a leaden-white sun,
The peoples of history, ancient and modern.

Charles Baudelaire

Le Mort joyeux

Dans une terre grasse et pleine d'escargots
Je veux creuser moi-même une fosse profonde,
Où je puisse à loisir étaler mes vieux os
Et dormir dans l'oubli comme un requin dans l'onde.

Je hais les testaments et je hais les tombeaux;
Plutôt que d'implorer une larme au monde,
Vivant, j'aimerais mieux inviter les corbeaux
A saigner tous les bouts de ma carcasse immonde.

O vers! noirs compagnons sans oreille et sans yeux,
Voyez venir à vous un mort libre et joyeux;
Philosophes viveurs, fils de la pourriture,

A travers ma ruine allez donc sans remords,
Et dites-moi s'il est encor quelque torture
Pour ce vieux corps sans âme et mort parmi les morts.

The Happy Corpse

Somewhere in rich, fertile earth full of snails
I will dig with my own hands a pit wide and deep,
In which I can calmly stretch out my old bones
And sleep in oblivion like a shark in the wave.

No testaments, no mausoleums for me;
Rather than plead with the world for a tear,
I'd prefer, still alive, to beckon the crows
Every inch of my vile, filthy carcass to bleed.

O worms! dark companions with no ear nor eye,
To you now comes a dead man who's happy and free;
Epicurean philosophers, scions of decay,

Feel free then to bore through my ruins at will,
And tell me if some torment still lies in store
For this soulless old body, more dead than alive.

Charles Baudelaire

La Cloche Fêlée

Il est amer et doux, pendant les nuits d'hiver,
D'écouter, près du feu qui palpite et qui fume,
Les souvenirs lointains lentement s'élever
Au bruit des carillons qui chantent dans la brume.

Bienheureuse la cloche au gosier vigoureux
Qui, malgré sa vieillesse, alerte et bien portante,
Jette fidèlement son cri religieux,
Ainsi qu'un vieux soldat qui veille sous la tente!

Moi, mon âme est fêlée, et lorsqu'en ses ennuis
Elle veut de ses chants peupler l'air froid des nuits,
Il arrive souvent que sa voix affaiblie

Semble le râle épais d'un blessé qu'on oublie
Au bord d'un lac de sang, sous un grand tas de morts,
Et qui meurt, sans bouger, dans d'immenses efforts.

The Cracked Bell

It is bitter and sweet, during cold winter nights,
To attend, by a fire that crackles and smokes,
As dim, distant memories are slowly called up
By the sound of bell-chimes ringing clear in the fog.

Thrice blessèd the bell with the vigorous throat,
Still spry, sound and healthy in spite of its age,
Which sings out its dutiful paean to God
Like a trusty old soldier on sentinel watch!

As for me, my soul's cracked, and when in its pain
It would people with anthems the night's frosty air,
There often are times when its weakened voice seems

Like the thick mortal gasp of a wounded man left
Near a huge pool of blood, in a great heap of dead,
Who is dying transfixed, every muscle astrain.

Spleen (I)

Pluviôse, irrité contre la ville entière,
De son urne à grands flots verse un froid ténébreux
Aux pâles habitants du voisin cimetière
Et la mortalité sur les faubourgs brumeux.

Mon chat sur le carreau cherchant une litière
Agite sans repos son corps maigre et galeux;
L'âme d'un vieux poëte erre dans la gouttière
Avec la triste voix d'un fantôme frileux.

Le bourdon se lamente, et la bûche enfumée
Accompagne en fausset la pendule enrhumée,
Cependant qu'en un jeu plein de sales parfums,

Héritage fatal d'une vieille hydropique,
Le beau valet de cœur et la dame de pique
Causent sinistrement de leurs amours défunts.

Late January

Pluviôse,* sorely vexed with the town as a whole,
From his urn pours out copious drafts of dark cold
For the neighboring churchyard's inhabitants pale
And mortality over the foggy faubourgs.

My cat, gaunt and mangy, keeps circling about,
Trying vainly to find a soft bed on the tile;
An old poet's soul prowls the rainspout and wails
With the querulous voice of a shivering wraith.

The great bell laments, and the smoky log whines
Obbligato falsetto to the clock's rheumy wheeze,
While in a deck of cards that reeks of cheap perfumes,

Some dropsical old woman's mortal legacy,
The handsome knave of hearts and the queen of spades
Chat surreptitiously of their defunct amours.

* Pluviôse: a winter month of France's short-lived Revolutionary calendar.

Spleen (II)

J'ai plus de souvenirs que si j'avais mille ans.

Un gros meuble à tiroirs encombrés de bilans,
De vers, de billets doux, de procès, de romances,
Avec de lourds cheveux roulés dans des quittances,
Cache moins de secrets que mon triste cerveau.
C'est une pyramide, un immense caveau,
Qui contient plus de morts que la fosse commune.

—Je suis un cimetière abhorré de la lune,
Où comme des remords, se traînent de longs vers
Qui s'acharnent toujours sur mes morts les plus chers.
Je suis un vieux boudoir plein de roses fanées,
Où gît tout un fouillis de modes surannées,
Où les pastels plaintifs et les pâles Boucher,
Seuls, respirent l'odeur d'un flacon débouché.

Rien n'égale en longueur les boiteuses journées,
Quand, sous les lourds flocons des neigeuses années,
L'ennui, fruit de la morne incuriosité,
Prend les proportions de l'immortalité.
—Désormais tu n'es plus, ô matière vivante!
Qu'un granit entouré d'une vague épouvante,
Assoupi dans le fond d'un Sahara brumeux;
Un vieux sphinx ignoré du monde insoucieux,
Oublié sur la carte, et dont l'humeur farouche
Ne chante qu'aux rayons du soleil qui se couche!

The Sphinx

I've more memories than were I a thousand years old.

A great chest of drawers, crammed full of accounts,
Of verses, love-letters, law-papers, songs,
With thick locks of hair rolled up in receipts,
Hides away fewer secrets than my wretched brain.
It's a pyramid, a catacomb vaulted and vast,
Wherein corpses lie thicker than in potter's field.

—I am a cemetery shunned by the moon,
Where like pangs of remorse, long worms crawl about,
Ever eating away at my most cherished dead.
I'm a fusty boudoir full of roses all sere,
Where lies strewn a great jumble of outmoded gowns,
Where pale Boucher portraits and plaintive pastels
Breathe lonely the scent from an unstoppered vial.

There is nothing so long as the slow-limping days,
Those ponderous snowflakes that drift into years,
When ennui, the offspring of glum apathy,
Takes on the dimensions of immortality.
—O live flesh and blood! thou art henceforth no more
Than an outcrop of granite beset by vague terror,
Languishing deep in some hazy Sahara;
An old sphinx unmarked by the indifferent world,
Unmapped and forgotten, whose peevishness sings
To none save the rays of the westering sun!

Spleen (III)

Je suis comme le roi d'un pays pluvieux,
Riche, mais impuissant, jeune et pourtant très-vieux,
Qui, de ses précepteurs méprisant les courbettes,
S'ennuie avec ses chiens comme avec d'autres bêtes.
Rien ne peut l'égayer, ni gibier, ni faucon,
Ni son peuple mourant en face du balcon.
Du bouffon favori la grotesque ballade
Ne distrait plus le front de ce cruel malade;
Son lit fleurdelisé se transforme en tombeau,
Et les dames d'atour, pour qui tout prince est beau,
Ne savent plus trouver l'impudique toilette
Pour tirer un souris de ce jeune squelette.
Le savant qui lui fait de l'or n'a jamais pu
De son être extirper l'élément corrompu,
Et dans ces bains de sang qui des Romains nous viennent
Et dont sur leurs vieux jours les puissants se souviennent,
Il n'a su réchauffer ce cadavre hébété
Où coule au lieu de sang l'eau verte du Léthé.

Taedium vitae

I am like the king of some pluvious land,
Wealthy, but powerless, young and yet decrepit,
Who scorns his preceptors' obsequious bows
And is bored with his dogs as with other dumb brutes.
Nothing can cheer him—not hunting, nor falconry,
Nor his people groveling before the balcony.
The grotesque ballade of his favorite buffoon
No longer amuses this sick, cruel man;
His fleur-de-lys bed has turned into a bier,
And the ladies at court, who deem any prince fair,
No longer can find the provocative gown
To elicit a smile from this young skeleton.
The sage who makes gold for him hasn't known how
To distill the base element out of his soul;
And in blood-baths, for which we've the Romans to thank,
And which despots remember when feeling their age,
He has failed to warm up that benumbed, lifeless corpse
Through which flows not blood, but Lethe's green flood.

Spleen (IV)

Quand le ciel bas et lourd pèse comme un couvercle
Sur l'esprit gémissant en proie aux longs ennuis,
Et que de l'horizon embrassant tout le cercle
Il nous verse un jour noir plus triste que les nuits;

Quand la terre est changée en un cachot humide,
Où l'Espérance, comme une chauve-souris,
S'en va battant les murs de son aile timide
Et se cognant la tête à des plafonds pourris;

Quand la pluie étalant ses immenses traînées,
D'une vaste prison imite les barreaux,
Et qu'un peuple muet d'infâmes araignées
Vient tendre ses filets au fond de nos cerveaux,

Des cloches tout à coup sautent avec furie
Et lancent vers le ciel un affreux hurlement,
Ainsi que des esprits errants et sans patrie
Qui se mettent à geindre opiniâtrément.

—Et de longs corbillards, sans tambours ni musique,
Défilent lentement dans mon âme; l'Espoir,
Vaincu, pleure, et l'Angoisse atroce, despotique,
Sur mon crâne incliné plante son drapeau noir.

Despair

When the low, leaden sky presses down like a lid
On the suffering spirit in endless travail,
And when from around the horizon's whole rim
It pours us dark daylight more somber than night;

When the earth is turned into a dank dungeon cell
Wherein Hope, like a fluttering bat in the gloom,
In vain beats the walls with a timorous wing
And bruises her head on the ceiling's foul slime;

When rain, hanging out its immense sweeping trains,
Resembles a vast, murky prison's thick bars,
And a host of vile spiders soundlessly come
To spin their damp webs in the depths of our brains,

Then bells, of a sudden, explode in a rage
And fling toward the heavens a dolorous cry,
Like wandering spirits in search of a home,
Beginning an obstinate, whiny complaint.

—And in silent cortège, without music or drums,
Long black hearses dead-slowly defile in my soul;
Hope, vanquished, weeps; and fierce Anguish, despotic,
Upon my bowed skull firmly plants her black flag.

Obsession

Grands bois, vous m'effrayez comme des cathédrales;
Vous hurlez comme l'orgue; et dans nos cœurs maudits,
Chambres d'éternel deuil où vibrent de vieux râles,
Répondent les échos de vos De profundis.

Je te hais, Océan! tes bonds et tes tumultes,
Mon esprit les retrouve en lui; ce rire amer
De l'homme vaincu, plein de sanglots et d'insultes,
Je l'entends dans le rire énorme de la mer.

Comme tu me plairais, ô nuit! sans ces étoiles
Dont la lumière parle un langage connu!
Car je cherche le vide, et le noir, et le nu!

Mais les ténèbres sont elles-mêmes des toiles
Où vivent, jaillissant de mon œil par milliers,
Des êtres disparus aux regards familiers.

Obsession

Great forests, you daunt me as cathedrals do;
You shout like the organ; and in our stricken hearts,
Mourning-chambers where ceaselessly quaver old rales,
The echoes of your De profundis resound.

Vast Ocean, I hate you! Your turmoil and heave
My spirit within itself finds; that bitter laugh
Of the defeated man, fraught with sobs and affronts,
I can hear in the monstrous guffaw of the sea.

How you'd please me, O Night, were it not for those stars,
Whose light speaks a language I know! For I seek
Nothing more than the void, and the featureless dark!

But the darkness itself is a canvas whereon,
Erupting by thousands from out of my eye,
Spring to life recognizable, long-vanished souls.

Le Goût du néant

Morne esprit, autrefois amoureux de la lutte,
L'Espoir, dont l'éperon attisait ton ardeur,
Ne veut plus t'enfourcher! Couche-toi sans pudeur,
Vieux cheval dont le pied à chaque obstacle bute.

Résigne-toi, mon cœur; dors ton sommeil de brute.

Esprit vaincu, fourbu! Pour toi, vieux maraudeur,
L'amour n'a plus de goût, non plus que la dispute;
Adieu donc, chants du cuivre et soupirs de la flûte!
Plaisirs, ne tentez plus un cœur sombre et boudeur!

Le Printemps adorable a perdu son odeur!

Et le Temps m'engloutit minute par minute,
Comme la neige immense un corps pris de roideur;
Je contemple d'en haut le globe en sa rondeur
Et je n'y cherche plus l'abri d'une cahute.

Avalanche, veux-tu m'emporter dans ta chute?

A Taste for Oblivion

Wretched spirit, once eager the battle to join,
Thy old rider Hope, whose spur fanned thy flame,
Will no longer mount thee! Lie down without shame,
Old war-horse who stumbles at every loose stone.

Resign thyself, heart; sleep thy dumb-brutish sleep.

Broken-down, foundered spirit! Old charger, for thee
There's no savor in love any more, nor dispute;
So farewell, singing brass and soft, sighing flute!
Delights, tempt no more a morose, sullen heart!

The adored goddess Springtime her fragrance has lost!

And minute by minute I'm swallowed by Time,
As a stiffening corpse is engulfed by vast snow;
I behold from aloft the whole round of the globe
And I no longer look for a sheltering wall.

Avalanche, wilt thou sweep me away in thy fall?

L'Héautontimorouménos

Je te frapperai sans colère
Et sans haine, comme un boucher,
Comme Moïse le rocher!
Et je ferai de ta paupière,

Pour abreuver mon Saharah,
Jaillir les eaux de la souffrance.
Mon désir gonflé d'espérance
Sur tes pleurs salés nagera

Comme un vaisseau qui prend le large,
Et dans mon cœur qu'ils soûleront
Tes chers sanglots retentiront
Comme un tambour qui bat la charge!

Ne suis-je pas un faux accord
Dans la divine symphonie,
Grâce à la vorace Ironie
Qui me secoue et qui me mord?

Elle est dans ma voix, la criarde!
C'est tout mon sang, ce poison noir!
Je suis le sinistre miroir
Où la mégère se regarde!

Je suis la plaie et le couteau!
Je suis le soufflet et la joue!
Je suis les membres et la roue,
Et la victime et le bourreau!

Charles Baudelaire

The Self-Tormentor

I'll strike you coldly, without hate
Or anger, as a butcher strikes,
As Moses smote the Horeb rock!
And from your lids I'll make gush forth,

To irrigate my Sahará,
The floods of suffering and pain.
My hot desire, blown large by hope,
Will swim upon your salt tears like

A ship that's putting out to sea,
And in my heart, made drunk thereby,
Your cherished sobs will echo like
A drum that's beating out the charge!

Am I not a discordant note
In God's celestial symphony,
Thanks to voracious Irony
Who bites and shakes me in her jaws?

She's in my voice, the strident scold!
It's all my blood, this poison black!
I am the mirror sinister
Wherein the shrew regards herself!

I am the stab-wound and the knife!
I am the stung cheek and the slap!
I am the members and the wheel,
The victim and the hangman too!

Charles Baudelaire

Je suis de mon cœur le vampire,
—Un de ces grands abandonnés
Au rire éternel condamnés,
Et qui ne peuvent plus sourire!

I am the vampire of my heart,
—One of those great forsaken few
Condemned eternally to laugh,
And able nevermore to smile!

L'Horloge

Horloge! dieu sinistre, effrayant, impassible,
Dont le doigt nous menace et nous dit: "Souviens-toi!"
Les vibrantes Douleurs dans ton cœur plein d'effroi
Se planteront bientôt comme dans une cible;

Le Plaisir vaporeux fuira vers l'horizon
Ainsi qu'une sylphide au fond de la coulisse;
Chaque instant te dévore un morceau du délice
A chaque homme accordé pour toute sa saison.

Trois mille six cents fois par heure, la Seconde
Chuchote: *Souviens-toi!* —Rapide, avec sa voix
D'insecte, Maintenant dit: Je suis Autrefois,
Et j'ai pompé ta vie avec ma trompe immonde!

Remember! Souviens-toi! prodigue! *Esto memor!*
(Mon gosier de métal parle toutes les langues!)
Les minutes, mortel folâtre, sont des gangues
Qu'il ne faut pas lâcher sans en extraire l'or!

Souviens-toi que le Temps est un joueur avide
Qui gagne sans tricher, à tout coup! c'est la loi.
Le jour décroît; la nuit augmente; souviens-toi!
Le gouffre a toujours soif; la clepsydre se vide.

Tantôt sonnera l'heure où le divin Hasard,
Où l'auguste Vertu, ton épouse encor vierge,
Où le Repentir même (oh! la dernière auberge!)
Où tout te dira: "Meurs, vieux lâche! il est trop tard!"

Charles Baudelaire

The Clock

O Clock! thou impassive, dread, sinister god,
Whose menacing finger "Remember!" exhorts,
The shattering Griefs that thy fearsome heart holds
Will soon, like winged shafts in a target, strike home!

Ephemeral Pleasure will fade from the scene
As a sylphid flees offstage and into the wings;
Each moment devours one more portion of those
Sweet delights meted out for his lifetime to each.

Three thousand six hundred times every hour,
The Second still whispers: "Remember!" Swift Now,
With its insect-like voice, ticks out: "I am the Past,
And my filthy proboscis has sucked out thy life!"

Souviens-toi! Remember! Wastrel! *Esto memor!*
(My gullet of metal speaks all the world's tongues!)
Feckless mortal, the minutes are matrices, gangues,
Which must not be let go without yielding their gold!

Remember that Time is a dice-player keen
Who wins without fraud, every cast! That's the law.
The day wanes; the night waxes; remember! The pit
Is forever athirst, and the clepsydra drains.

The hour will soon strike when omnipotent Chance,
When radiant Virtue, thy still-virgin spouse,
When Repentance itself (ah—the last wayside inn!),
When all will say: "Die, old poltroon! It's too late!"

Charles Baudelaire

Paysage

Je veux, pour composer chastement mes églogues,
Coucher auprès du ciel, comme les astrologues,
Et, voisin des clochers, écouter en rêvant
Leurs hymnes solennels emportés par le vent.
Les deux mains au menton, du haut de ma mansarde,
Je verrai l'atelier qui chante et qui bavarde;
Les tuyaux, les clochers, ces mâts de la cité,
Et les grands ciels qui font rêver d'éternité.

Il est doux, à travers les brumes, de voir naître
L'étoile dans l'azur, la lampe à la fenêtre,
Les fleuves de charbon monter au firmament
Et la lune verser son pâle enchantement.

Je verrai les printemps, les étés, les automnes;
Et quand viendra l'hiver aux neiges monotones,
Je fermerai partout portières et volets
Pour bâtir dans la nuit mes féeriques palais.
Alors je rêverai des horizons bleuâtres,
Des jardins, des jets d'eau pleurant dans les albâtres,
Des baisers, des oiseaux chantant soir et matin,
Et tout ce que l'Idylle a de plus enfantin.
L'Emeute, tempêtant vainement à ma vitre,
Ne fera pas lever mon front de mon pupitre;
Car je serai plongé dans cette volupté,
D'évoquer le Printemps avec ma volonté,
De tirer un soleil de mon cœur, et de faire
De mes pensers brûlants une tiède atmosphère.

Landscape

I want, in which chastely my eclogues to pen,
A room near the sky, such as star-gazers have,
Where I'll listen and dream as my neighbors, the bells,
Waft forth on the wind their devout, solemn hymns.
Gazing out, chin in hands, from my garret on high,
I'll see ateliers humming with chatter and song;
Smoke-stacks and church-spires, the city's tall masts,
And the heavens evoking eternity's dreams.

It is lovely to watch, through the haze, as each star
Is born in the blue, in each window a lamp;
As the rivers of soot to the firmament rise,
And the moon's pale enchantment is cast over all.

I shall see springtimes, and summers, and falls,
And when winter sets in with its tedious snows,
I shall close all door-curtains and shutters, and then
I shall build in the night fairy castles in Spain.
I shall dream then of distant horizons blue-grey,
Of gardens, of white marble fountains that weep.
Of kisses, of birds singing morning and eve,
And of all that's most childlike in Idyll's romance.
Though Riot be raging outside in the street,
I shall not even lift up my head from my desk;
For I'll be enrapt in the utter delight
Of conjuring Spring by the strength of my will,
Extracting a sun from my heart, and with thoughts
That burn hotly, creating a warm atmosphere.

Charles Baudelaire

Le Soleil

Le long du vieux faubourg, où pendent aux masures
Les persiennes, abri des secrètes luxures,
Quand le soleil cruel frappe à traits redoublés
Sur la ville et les champs, sur les toits et les blés,
Je vais m'exercer seul à ma fantasque escrime,
Flairant dans tous les coins les hasards de la rime,
Trébuchant sur les mots comme sur les pavés,
Heurtant parfois des vers depuis longtemps rêvés.

Ce père nourricier, ennemi des chloroses,
Eveille dans les champs les vers comme les roses;
Il fait s'évaporer les soucis vers le ciel,
Et remplit les cerveaux et les ruches de miel.
C'est lui qui rajeunit les porteurs de béquilles
Et les rend gais et doux comme des jeunes filles,
Et commande aux moissons de croître et de mûrir
Dans le cœur immortel qui toujours veut fleurir!

Quand, ainsi qu'un poète, il descend dans les villes,
Il ennoblit le sort des choses les plus viles,
Et s'introduit en roi, sans bruit et sans valets,
Dans tous les hôpitaux et dans tous les palais.

The Sun

Through the old part of town, where on cottages hang
Heavy shutters, a screen for clandestine debauch,
When the sun beats down fiercely with supercharged rays
Upon city and countryside, rooftops and crops,
I go poetry-fencing, my own fancy's game,
In all corners *en garde* against dangers of rhyme,
Stumbling over words as on loose paving-stones,
And sometimes upon lines heard long since in my dreams.

That benign foster-father, chloroses' great foe,
Wakens verses, like roses, from sleep in the fields;
He evaporates cares, turns them into thin air;
He fills bee-hives with honey and brains with ideas.
It is he who restores to crutch-bearers their youth
And makes them as gentle and gay as young girls.
He commands all the crops to grow tall and mature
In their immortal hearts, which would rather just bloom!

When he comes, like a poet, down into a town,
He ennobles the fate of the lowliest things,
And like a good king, without fanfare or suite,
Penetrates every poorhouse and every chateau.

Les Sept Vieillards

Fourmillante cité, cité pleine de rêves,
Où le spectre, en plein jour, raccroche le passant!
Les mystères partout coulent comme des sèves
Dans les canaux étroits du colosse puissant.

Un matin, cependant que dans la triste rue
Les maisons, dont la brume allongeait la hauteur,
Simulaient les deux quais d'une rivière accrue,
Et que, décor semblable à l'âme de l'acteur,

Un brouillard sale et jaune inondait tout l'espace,
Je suivais, roidissant mes nerfs comme un héros
Et discutant avec mon âme déjà lasse,
Le faubourg secoué par les lourds tombereaux.

Tout à coup, un vieillard dont les guenilles jaunes
Imitaient la couleur de ce ciel pluvieux,
Et dont l'aspect aurait fait pleuvoir les aumônes,
Sans la méchanceté qui luisait dans ses yeux,

M'apparut. On eût dit sa prunelle trempée
Dans le fiel; son regard aiguisait les frimas,
Et sa barbe à longs poils, roide comme une épée,
Se projetait, pareille à celle de Judas.

Il n'était pas voûté, mais cassé, son échine
Faisant avec sa jambe un parfait angle droit,
Si bien que son bâton, parachevant sa mine,
Lui donnait la tournure et le pas maladroit

Charles Baudelaire

The Seven Old Men

City teeming with life, city pregnant with dreams,
Where ghosts, in broad daylight, accost passers-by!
Eerie mysteries flow like tree-sap everywhere
Through the mighty colossus's strait passageways.

One morning, when buildings on drab, dismal streets,
Looming taller by half in the mist-laden air,
Simulated the banks of a river in flood,
And when, a décor like the thespian's soul,

An unclean yellow fog inundated all space,
I was walking, rehearsing my soul's weary woes,
And heroically steeling my nerves to the noise
And vibration of garbage-carts rumbling by.

Suddenly an old man, clad in yellowish rags
Imitating the hue of that pluvious sky,
And whose looks would have earned him a shower of alms
Had there not been a venomous glint in his eye,

Stood before me. His eyes, you'd have said, were adrip
With malice: their glance put an edge on the cold;
And his whiskers, long-haired and as stiff as a sword,
Jutted out from his face, like foul Judas's beard.

He was not merely bent, but quite broken: his spine
With his leg made a perfect right angle, and this,
With his stick to top off the effect of his mien,
Made him look as ungainly of figure and gait

D'un quadrupède infirme ou d'un juif à trois pattes.
Dans la neige et la boue il allait s'empêtrant,
Comme s'il écrasait des morts sous ses savates,
Hostile à l'univers plutôt qu'indifférent.

Son pareil le suivait: barbe, œil, dos, bâton, loques,
Nul trait ne distinguait, du même enfer venu,
Ce jumeau centenaire, et ces spectres baroques
Marchaient du même pas vers un but inconnu.

A quel complot infâme étais-je donc en butte,
Ou quel méchant hasard ainsi m'humiliait?
Car je comptai sept fois, de minute en minute,
Ce sinistre vieillard qui se multipliait!

Que celui-là qui rit de mon inquiétude,
Et qui n'est pas saisi d'un frisson fraternel,
Songe bien que malgré tant de décrepitude
Ces sept monstres hideux avaient l'air éternel!

Aurais-je, sans mourir, contemplé le huitième,
Sosie inexorable, ironique et fatal,
Dégoûtant Phénix, fils et père de lui-même?
—Mais je tournai le dos au cortège infernal.

Exaspéré comme un ivrogne qui voit double,
Je rentrai, je fermai ma porte, épouvanté,
Malade et morfondu, l'esprit fiévreux et trouble,
Blessé par le mystère et par l'absurdité!

Vainement ma raison voulait prendre la barre;
La tempête en jouant déroutait ses efforts,
Et mon âme dansait, dansait, vieille gabarre
Sans mâts, sur une mer monstrueuse et sans bords!

As a lame quadruped or a three-legged Jew.
He went slogging along in the snow and the mud
As if trampling dead bodies beneath his old shoes—
To the universe hostile, not indifferent.

After him came his double: beard, eye, back, stick, rags—
Not a single trait differed in this perfect twin
Centenarian from the same hell, and in step
These weird specters marched off, destination unknown.

By what infamous plot was I victimized here,
Or by what foul mischance to such horror exposed?
For I counted, from minute to minute, five more,
As that sinister oldster was cloned sevenfold!

Let whoso is amused at my anxiety
And not seized with a brotherly shudder, take note
That these hideous monsters, all seven, despite
Their decrepitude, looked quite immortal to me!

Could I have survived, had I sighted an eighth—
Implacable Sosia, ironic, *fatal,*
Or revolting Phœníx, his own father and son?
But I turned my back on the infernal cortège.

Mortified as a drunk seeing double, I fled
Back behind my locked door, terror-stricken, aghast,
Feeling nauseous, feverish, chilled to the bone,
My mind wounded, undone by enigma and farce.

In vain did my reason try taking the helm;
The storm raging on caused its efforts to fail,
And my soul, an old barge without masts, helplessly
Pitched and tossed on a monstrous and limitless sea!

Charles Baudelaire

Les Aveugles

Contemple-les, mon âme; ils sont vraiment affreux!
Pareils aux mannequins; vaguement ridicules;
Terribles, singuliers comme les somnambules;
Dardant on ne sait où leurs globes ténébreux.

Leurs yeux, d'où la divine étincelle est partie,
Comme s'ils regardaient au loin, restent levés
Au ciel; on ne les voit jamais vers les pavés
Pencher rêveusement leur tête appesantie.

Ils traversent ainsi le noir illimité,
Ce frère du silence éternel. O cité!
Pendant qu'autour de nous tu chantes, ris et beugles,

Eprise du plaisir jusqu'à l'atrocité,
Vois! je me traîne aussi! mais, plus qu'eux hébété,
Je dis: Que cherchent-ils au Ciel, tous ces aveugles?

The Blind

Behold them, my soul; how ghastly they are!
Like mannequins, vaguely ridiculous, stiff;
Like sleep-walkers, frightening, eerie, bizarre;
Rolling their sightless orbs this way and that.

Their eyes, from which the divine spark is fled,
As if gazing afar, remain raised to the sky;
You never see one of them hanging his head
Heavily, musingly down toward the street.

They traverse in this fashion the limitless dark,
That twin of eternal silence. O city!
While you all around us laugh, bellow and sing,

So madly enamored of pleasure—look here!
I too shuffle along! But bemused more than they,
I say: What seek they in Heaven, all these blind?

Charles Baudelaire

Une Passante

La rue assourdissante autour de moi hurlait.
Longue, mince, en grand deuil, douleur majestueuse,
Une femme passa, d'une main fastueuse
Soulevant, balançant le feston et l'ourlet;

Agile et noble, avec sa jambe de statue.
Moi, je buvais, crispé comme un extravagant,
Dans son œil, ciel livide où germe l'ouragan,
La douceur qui fascine et le plaisir qui tue.

Un éclair . . . puis la nuit! —Fugitive beauté
Dont le regard m'a fait soudainement renaître,
Ne te verrai-je plus que dans l'éternité?

Ailleurs, bien loin d'ici! trop tard! jamais peut-être!
Car j'ignore où tu fuis, tu ne sais où je vais,
O toi que j'eusse aimée, ô toi qui le savais!

Charles Baudelaire

A Woman Passing By

All around roared the deafening din of the street.
Tall, slim, in deep mourning, majestic in grief,
A woman walked by, with one sumptuous hand
Uplifting and swinging festoon and stitched hem;

Light-footed, patrician, of statuesque limb.
As for me, mouth agape like a fool, I drank in
From her eyes, livid sky where the hurricane brews,
The sweetness that charms and the pleasure that kills.

One bolt—then the dark! Evanescent beauty
At whose glance I was suddenly born anew,
Shall I see you no more save in some after-life?

Far away! Or too late! Or perhaps nevermore!
I know not where you flee, nor you where I go,
O you I would have loved, you who knew it was so!

to,

205

Charles Baudelaire

Le Crépuscule du soir

Voici le soir charmant, ami du criminel;
Il vient comme un complice, à pas de loup; le ciel
Se ferme lentement comme une grande alcôve,
Et l'homme impatient se change en bête fauve.

O soir, aimable soir, désiré par celui
Dont les bras, sans mentir, peuvent dire: Aujourd'hui
Nous avons travaillé! —C'est le soir qui soulage
Les esprits que dévore une douleur sauvage,
Le savant obstiné dont le front s'alourdit,
Et l'ouvrier courbé qui regagne son lit.
Cependant des démons malsains dans l'atmosphère
S'éveillent lourdement, comme des gens d'affaire,
Et cognent en volant les volets et l'auvent.
A travers les lueurs que tourmente le vent
La prostitution s'allume dans les rues;
Comme une fourmilière elle ouvre ses issues;
Partout elle se fraye un occulte chemin,
Ainsi que l'ennemi qui tente un coup de main;
Elle remue au sein de la cité de fange
Comme un ver qui dérobe à l'Homme ce qu'il mange.
On entend çà et là les cuisines siffler,
Les théâtres glapir, les orchestres ronfler;
Les tables d'hôte, dont le jeu fait les délices,
S'emplissent de catins et d'escrocs, leurs complices,
Et les voleurs, qui n'ont ni trêve ni merci,
Vont bientôt commencer leur travail, eux aussi,
Et forcer doucement les portes et les caisses
Pour vivre quelques jours et vêtir leurs maîtresses.

Nightfall

Now here's charming evening, the criminal's friend;
Stealthily, like an accomplice, it comes;
The skies slowly close like a great alcove-bed,
And man just can't wait to become a wild beast.

O evening, dear evening, so longed for by him
Whose two arms can truthfully say, "Today
We have labored!" —It's evening that brings sweet relief
To spirits devoured by a desperate grief,
To the painstaking scholar with dull, aching brow
And the bone-weary worker regaining his bed.
But meanwhile, foul demons abroad in the air
Awaken lethargic, like men of affairs,
And fly about banging on shutters and eaves.
As the wind swoops down on the darkening streets,
Prostitution lights up with its lurid gleams;
Like an anthill it opens its outlet holes;
It makes its way secretly everywhere,
Like the enemy massing to mount an attack;
It stirs in the bowels of the precincts of vice
Like a tapeworm usurping the food humans eat.
Here and there one hears kitchens sizzle and hiss,
Theaters yammer and orchestras blare;
Supper clubs, where it's gambling that's all the rage,
Are filling with bawds and their allies, the crooks;
And ubiquitous burglars, who never call truce,
They likewise will shortly be setting to work,
Surreptitiously jimmying doors and tills
To subsist a few days and to dress up their jills.

Recueille-toi, mon âme, en ce grave moment,
Et ferme ton oreille à ce rugissement.
C'est l'heure où les douleurs des malades s'aigrissent!
La sombre Nuit les prend à la gorge; ils finissent
Leur destinée et vont vers le gouffre commun;
L'hôpital se remplit de leurs soupirs. —Plus d'un
Ne viendra plus chercher la soupe parfumée,
Au coin du feu, le soir, auprès d'une âme aimée.

Encore la plupart n'ont-ils jamais connu
La douceur du foyer et n'ont jamais vécu!

Reflect, O my soul, at this fateful hour,
And turn a deaf ear to its racketing roar.
It's the time when the pains of the stricken grow sharp!
Somber Night grips them now by the throat; they live out
Their span and draw near to the common abyss;
The hospital's filled with their sighs. —More than one
Will come never again to share savory soup
By the fire, in the evening, with some beloved soul.

Why, most of them never even have known
The sweetness of home, and have never lived!

Charles Baudelaire

L'Amour du mensonge

Quand je te vois passer, ô ma chère indolente,
Au chant des instruments qui se brise au plafond
Suspendant ton allure harmonieuse et lente,
Et promenant l'ennui de ton regard profond;

Quand je contemple, aux feux du gaz qui le colore,
Ton front pâle, embelli par un morbide attrait,
Où les torches du soir allument une aurore,
Et tes yeux attirants comme ceux d'un portrait,

Je me dis: Qu'elle est belle! et bizarrement fraîche!
Le souvenir massif, royale et lourde tour,
La couronne, et son cœur, meurtri comme une pêche,
Est mûr, comme son corps, pour le savant amour.

Es-tu le fruit d'automne aux saveurs souveraines?
Es-tu vase funèbre attendant quelques pleurs,
Parfum qui fait rêver aux oasis lointaines,
Oreiller caressant, ou corbeille de fleurs?

Je sais qu'il est des yeux, des plus mélancoliques,
Qui ne recèlent point de secrets précieux;
Beaux écrins sans joyaux, médaillons sans reliques,
Plus vides, plus profonds que vous-mêmes, ô Cieux!

Mais ne suffit-il pas que tu sois l'apparence,
Pour réjouir un cœur qui fuit la vérité?
Qu'importe ta bêtise ou ton indifférence?
Masque ou décor, salut! J'adore ta beauté.

Charles Baudelaire

Love of the Lie

When I see you pass by, my dear indolent one,
As the music breaks up on the ceiling above
Suspending your slow, graceful movement, and then
Glancing 'round with that look of profoundest ennui;

When I contemplate, tinted with lights by the gas,
Your pale forehead, embellished by one beauty-spot,
Where the torches of evening are kindling a dawn,
And your eyes which like those of a portrait compel,

I think: How lovely she is! How strangely cool!
She is memory massive, a great royal tower,
The crown; and her heart, soft and bruised like a peach,
Is ripe, like her body, for sweet, knowing love.

Are you autumn's late fruit with its flavors supreme?
A funeral vase that's awaiting some tears?
A perfume that stirs dreams of oases remote,
A pillow's caress, or a basket of flowers?

I know there are eyes, of the most melancholy,
Which not even one precious secret conceal:
Jewel-cases sans gems, reliquaries sans bones,
More empty and deeper, O heavens, than yourselves!

But is outward appearance not all you need be
To bring joy to a heart that recoils from the truth?
So you're stupid, indifferent—what's that to me?
Mask or décor, all hail! I adore your beauty.

Charles Baudelaire

*   *   *

La servante au grand cœur dont vous étiez jalouse,
Et qui dort son sommeil sous une humble pelouse,
Nous devrions pourtant lui porter quelques fleurs.
Les morts, les pauvres morts, ont de grandes douleurs,
Et quand octobre souffle, émondeur des vieux arbres,
Son vent mélancolique à l'entour de leurs marbres,
Certe, ils doivent trouver les vivants bien ingrats,
A dormir, comme ils font, chaudement dans leurs draps,
Tandis que, dévorés de noires songeries,
Sans compagnon de lit, sans bonnes causeries,
Vieux squelettes gelés travaillés par le ver,
Ils sentent s'égoutter les neiges de l'hiver
Et le siècle couler, sans qu'amis ni famille
Remplacent les lambeaux qui pendent à leur grille.

Lorsque la bûche siffle et chante, si le soir,
Calme, dans le fauteuil, je la voyais s'asseoir,
Si, par une nuit bleue et froide de décembre,
Je la trouvais tapie en un coin de ma chambre,
Grave, et venant du fond de son lit éternel
Couver l'enfant grandi de son œil maternel,
Que pourrais-je répondre à cette âme pieuse,
Voyant tomber des pleurs de sa paupière creuse?

The Nanny

The great-hearted nanny whom you were jealous of ,
And who now sleeps beneath a humble patch of sod—
We really ought to take her flowers now and then.
The dead, poor things, have sorrows infinite to bear,
And when October, pruner of old trees, blows in
With mournful wind that moans around their marble stones,
They surely must find us, the living, ingrates all,
To sleep so snug and warm beneath our coverlets,
While they, the dead, consumed by bitter reveries,
With none to share their bed, with no good pillow-talk,
Outworn and frozen skeletons prey to the worm,
Are feeling winter snowfalls melt and drain away,
And seeing ages pass, while no kinfolk nor friends
Come to replace the tattered wreaths hung on their grilles.

If, when at dusk the fire-log sings and whines, I were
To see her sitting quietly in the big chair;
If, on some frosty-blue December night, I were
To find her huddled in a corner of my room,
Concerned, and coming from her deep eternal bed
To keep maternal watch over the grown-up child,
What could I find to say to that dear pious soul
On seeing teardrops falling from her sunken lids?

Brumes et pluies

O fins d'automne, hivers, printemps trempés de boue,
Endormeuses saisons! je vous aime et vous loue
D'envelopper ainsi mon cœur et mon cerveau
D'un linceul vaporeux et d'un vague tombeau.

Dans cette grande plaine où l'autan froid se joue,
Où par les longues nuits la girouette s'enroue,
Mon âme mieux qu'au temps du tiède renouveau
Ouvrira largement ses ailes de corbeau.

Rien n'est plus doux au cœur plein de choses funèbres,
Et sur qui dès longtemps descendent les frimas,
O blafardes saisons, reines de nos climats,

Que l'aspect permanent de vos pâles ténèbres,
—Si ce n'est, par un soir sans lune, deux à deux,
D'endormir la douleur sur un lit hasardeux.

Fogs and Rains

O late autumns, winters, mud-steeped early springs,
Soporiferous seasons! I love and praise you
For enwrapping my heart and my brain as you do
In a vaporous shroud and a kind of gray tomb.

On this great open plain where the cold storm-wind plays,
Where throughout the long nights the hoarse weather-vane rasps,
Far better than in the renewed warmth of spring,
My soul will spread amply its raven-black wings.

There is nothing more sweet to the heart full of woe
And long since encrusted with hoar-frost and rime,
O dull, dreary seasons, you queens of our clime,

Than the unchanging face of your colorless gloom—
Lest it be, on a dark moonless night, two by two,
To lull dolor to sleep on a casual bed.

Charles Baudelaire

Le Crépuscule du matin

La diane chantait dans les cours des casernes,
Et le vent du matin soufflait sur les lanternes.

C'était l'heure où l'essaim des rêves malfaisants
Tord sur leurs oreillers les bruns adolescents;
Où, comme un œil sanglant qui palpite et qui bouge,
La lampe sur le jour fait une tache rouge;
Où l'âme, sous le poids du corps revêche et lourd,
Imite les combats de la lampe et du jour.
Comme un visage en pleurs que les brises essuient,
L'air est plein du frisson des choses qui s'enfuient,
Et l'homme est las d'écrire et la femme d'aimer.

Les maisons çà et là commençaient à fumer.
Les femmes de plaisir, la paupière livide,
Bouche ouverte, dormaient de leur sommeil stupide;
Les pauvresses, traînant leurs seins maigres et froids,
Soufflaient sur leurs tisons et soufflaient sur leurs doigts.
C'était l'heure où parmi le froid et la lésine
S'aggravent les douleurs des femmes en gésine;
Comme un sanglot coupé par un sang écumeux
Le chant du coq au loin déchirait l'air brumeux;
Une mer de brouillards baignait les édifices,
Et les agonisants dans le fond des hospices
Poussaient leur dernier râle en hoquets inégaux.
Les débauchés rentraient, brisés par leurs travaux.

L'aurore grelottante en robe rose et verte
S'avançaient lentement sur la Seine déserte,
Et le sombre Paris, en se frottant les yeux,
Empoignait ses outils, vieillard laborieux.

Daybreak

The reveille sounded in barracks courtyards,
And the street-lamps flickered in the morning wind.

'Twas the hour when, plagued by troubling dreams,
Sun-browned adolescents writhe on their beds;
When the lamp, like a bloodshot and throbbing eye,
Makes a sickly red spot on the wan light of day;
When the soul, weighted down by the gross, fretful flesh,
Seems to struggle in vain, as the lamp with the day;
Like a face wet with tears being dried by the breeze,
The air brings a shudder, a keen sense of loss,
And man wearies of writing and woman of love.

Here and there, house-chimneys were starting to smoke.
Women of pleasure, livid-lidded, lay sprawled
With their mouths gaping open, in stupefied sleep;
Beggar-women, their scrawny, cold breasts a-droop,
Were blowing on embers and blowing on hands.
'Twas the hour when women in labor, amid
Deprivation and cold, feel more keenly their pains;
Like a sob interrupted by up-foaming blood,
A distant cock's crow ripped the mist-laden air;
The buildings all swam in an ocean of fog,
And the dying sequestered in old people's homes
Were breathing their last in irregular gasps.
Debauchees, worn out by their labors, crept home.

The shivering dawn, in pale pink and green dress,
Was slowly descending the deserted Seine,
And somber grey Paris, hard-working old man,
Was rubbing his eyes, laying hold of his tools.

Le Vin du solitaire

Le regard singulier d'une femme galante
Qui se glisse vers nous comme le rayon blanc
Que la lune onduleuse envoie au lac tremblant
Quand elle y veut baigner sa beauté nonchalante;

Le dernier sac d'écus dans les doigts d'un joueur;
Un baiser libertin de la maigre Adeline;
Les sons d'une musique énervante et câline,
Semblable au cri lointain de l'humaine douleur,

Tout cela ne vaut pas, ô bouteille profonde,
Les baumes pénétrants que ta panse féconde
Garde au cœur altéré du poëte pieux;

Tu lui verses l'espoir, la jeunesse et la vie,
—Et l'orgueil, ce trésor de toute gueuserie,
Qui nous rend triomphants et semblables aux Dieux!

Wine of the Lonely

A streetwalker's singular, meaningful glance
Which comes wriggling toward us as does the clear beam
That the undulant moon sends the trembling lake
When she chooses to bathe her cool beauty therein;

The last sack of crowns in a gambler's hand;
A hot, wanton kiss from a gaunt Adeline;
The cajoling of music, enervating and keen,
Like the age-old lament of humanity's pain—

All of this cannot match, O bottle profound,
The deep-healing balms that your bountiful bulge
Holds in store for the poet's devout, thirsty heart;

For him you pour hopefulness, youthfulness, life,
—And pride, that treasure in all wretchedness,
Which makes us triumphant and like unto Gods!

Les Deux Bonnes Sœurs

La Débauche et la Mort sont deux aimables filles,
Prodigues de baisers et riches de santé,
Dont le flanc toujours vierge et drapé de guenilles
Sous l'éternel labeur n'a jamais enfanté.

Au poète sinistre, ennemi des familles,
Favori de l'enfer, courtisan mal renté,
Tombeaux et lupanars montrent sous leurs charmilles
Un lit que le remords n'a jamais fréquenté.

Et la bière et l'alcôve en blasphèmes fécondes
Nous offrent tour à tour, comme deux bonnes sœurs,
De terribles plaisirs et d'affreuses douceurs.

Quand veux-tu m'enterrer, Débauche aux bras immondes?
O Mort, quand viendras-tu, sa rivale en attraits,
Sur ses myrtes infects enter tes noirs cyprès?

The Two Kind Sisters

Two amiable wenches are Debauchery and Death,
Prodigal with kisses and robust in health,
Whose flanks, ever virgin and draped in black rags,
Under labor eternal have never begot.

To the sinister poet, the family's foe,
The minion of Hell, the hard-up sycophant,
Bawdy-houses and tombs in their snug bowers show
A bed never haunted by pangs of remorse.

Both the bier and the alcove in blasphemies rich
To us offer in turn, like two sisters benign,
Calamitous pleasures and hideous ease.

O Debauch, when will thy filthy arms bury me?
O Death, when wilt thou, her great rival in charms,
Come to graft thy black cypress on her myrtles foul?

Charles Baudelaire

La Fontaine de sang

Il me semble parfois que mon sang coule à flots,
Ainsi qu'une fontaine aux rhythmiques sanglots.
Je l'entends bien qui coule avec un long murmure,
Mais je me tâte en vain pour trouver la blessure.

A travers la cité, comme dans un champ clos,
Il s'en va, transformant les pavés en îlots,
Désaltérant la soif de chaque créature,
Et partout colorant en rouge la nature.

J'ai demandé souvent à des vins captieux
D'endormir pour un jour la terreur qui me mine;
Le vin rend l'œil plus clair et l'oreille plus fine!

J'ai cherché dans l'amour un sommeil oublieux;
Mais l'amour n'est pour moi qu'un matelas d'aiguilles
Fait pour donner à boire à ces cruelles filles!

Charles Baudelaire

The Fountain of Blood

It sometimes seems to me that my blood's gushing out
As if from a rhythmically sobbing spring;
Quite clearly I hear its prolonged gurgling flow,
But in vain grope my body in search of the wound.

All over the city, as in a walled field,
It spreads, turning paving-stones into small isles,
Assuaging the thirst of each creature that lives,
And everywhere tincturing nature with red.

I have called many times upon strong, heady wines
To allay for a day the dull gnawing of fear;
The wine clears my eye and makes keener my ear!

I have sought in love an oblivious sleep;
But for me love is only a bed of nails
Designed to give drink to those cruel girls!

La Béatrice

Dans des terrains cendreux, calcinés, sans verdure,
Comme je me plaignais un jour à la nature,
Et que de ma pensée, en vaguant au hasard,
J'aiguisais lentement sur mon cœur le poignard,
Je vis en plein midi descendre sur ma tête
Un nuage funèbre et gros d'une tempête,
Qui portait un troupeau de démons vicieux,
Semblables à des nains cruels et curieux.
A me considérer froidement ils se mirent,
Et, comme des passants sur un fou qu'ils admirent,
Je les entendis rire et chuchoter entre eux,
En échangeant maint signe et maint clignement d'yeux:

—"Contemplons à loisir cette caricature
Et cette ombre d'Hamlet imitant sa posture,
Le regard indécis et les cheveux au vent.
N'est-ce pas grand'pitié de voir ce bon vivant,
Ce gueux, cet histrion en vacances, ce drôle,
Parce qu'il sait jouer artistement son rôle,
Vouloir intéresser au chant de ses douleurs
Les aigles, les grillons, les ruisseaux et les fleurs,
Et même à nous, auteurs de ces vieilles rubriques,
Réciter en hurlant ses tirades publiques?"

J'aurais pu (mon orgueil aussi haut que les monts
Domine la nuée et le cri des démons)
Détourner simplement ma tête souveraine,
Si je ne n'eusse pas vu parmi leur troupe obscène,
Crime qui n'a pas fait chanceler le soleil!
La reine de mon cœur au regard nonpareil,
Qui riait avec eux de ma sombre détresse
Et leur versait parfois quelque sale caresse.

The Beatrice

In a cindery wasteland, barren and sear,
As I was lamenting to Nature one day,
And as slowly, while wandering at random, I honed
The dagger of thought on that whetstone, my heart,
In broad daylight I saw coming down on my head
A great murky thundercloud, bearing along
A pack of foul demons, vicious of mien,
Like malevolent, cruel, inquisitive gnomes.
Coldly they started to give me the eye,
And like bystanders jeering a madman, I heard
How they snickered and whispered amongst themselves,
While exchanging sly nudges and many a wink.

"Let's have a good look at this caricature
And shadow of Hamlet, imitating his pose,
With irresolute gaze and wild, wind-tousled hair.
What a pity to see how this playboy, this scamp,
This impostor, this out-of-work actor, this rogue,
Just because he can act out his role with such flair
Tries to interest in hearing the tale of his woes
The eagles, the crickets, the flowers and the brooks,
And harangues even us, who devised these old tricks,
With his open-air ranting, his public tirades!"

I could have just turned my head proudly aside
(My pride, soaring high as the mountains, can rise
To dominate clouds and the howling of fiends),
If among that obscene crew I hadn't espied—
O crime! Yet the sun did not stagger nor reel!—
The queen of my heart with the nonpareil eyes,
Who was laughing with them at my somber distress
And favoring each with some sordid caress.

Charles Baudelaire

Le Reniement de St. Pierre

Qu'est-ce que Dieu fait donc de ce flot d'anathèmes
Qui monte tous les jours vers ses chers séraphins?
Comme un tyran gorgé de viandes et de vins,
Il s'endort au doux bruit de nos affreux blasphèmes.

Les sanglots des martyrs et des suppliciés
Sont une symphonie enivrante sans doute,
Puisque, malgré le sang que leur volupté coûte,
Les cieux ne s'en sont point encor rassasiés.

—Ah! Jésus! souviens-toi du jardin des Olives!
Dans ta simplicité tu priais à genoux
Celui qui dans son ciel riait au bruit de clous
Que d'ignobles bourreaux plantaient dans tes chairs vives.

Lorsque tu vis cracher sur ta divinité
La crapule du corps de garde et des cuisines,
Et lorsque tu sentis s'enfoncer les épines
Dans ton crâne où vivait l'immense Humanité;

Quand de ton corps brisé la pesanteur horrible
Allongeait tes deux bras distendus, que le sang
Et la sueur coulaient de ton front pâlissant,
Quand tu fus devant tous posé comme une cible,

Rêvais-tu de ces jours si brillants et si beaux
Où tu vins pour remplir l'éternelle promesse,
Où tu foulais, monté sur une douce ânesse,
Des chemins tout jonchés de fleurs et de rameaux,

St. Peter's Denial

So what does God do with the curses that rise
In a flood every day toward His dear seraphim?
Like a tyrant besotted with viands and wines,
He nods, lullabied by our blasphemous cries.

The sobs of the martyred, the screams from the rack
An enravishing symphony surely must be,
Since despite the blood shed for their pleasure thus far
The insatiable heavens still clamor for more.

Ah, Jesus! Remember Gethsemane's glade!
In your trusting simplicity, kneeling you prayed
To the One in His heaven who laughed at the sound
As base killers drove nails into your living flesh.

When you saw your divinity spat upon
By the riff-raff, the scum of the guard-house and streets;
When you felt the sharp thorns plunging into your head,
Wherein life for all vast Humanity lay;

When the terrible weight of your broken frame
Was stretching your overstrained arms, while blood
And sweat trickled down from your blanching brow;
When you hung there, a target of scorn for them all,

Did you dream of those beautiful, brilliant days
When you came the eternal promise to keep;
When astride a gentle she-donkey you trod
On ways all bestrewn with flowers and fronds;

Où, le cœur tout gonflé d'espoir et de vaillance,
Tu fouettais tous ces vils marchands à tour de bras,
Où tu fus maître enfin? Le remords n'a-t-il pas
Pénétré dans ton flanc plus avant que la lance?

Certes, je sortirai, quant à moi, satisfait
D'un monde où l'action n'est pas la sœur du rêve;
Puissé-je user du glaive et périr par le glaive.
Saint-Pierre a renié Jésus . . . il a bien fait!

When with heart swelled to bursting with courage and hope
You lashed those vile merchants with all your strength
And at last won the day? Did not, then, regret
Pierce your side even deeper than did the rude spear?

As for me, I shall be quite content to depart
From a world where the deed is not kin to the dream;
Let me live by the sword and die by the sword.
St. Peter denied Jesus—and he did right!

Charles Baudelaire

La Mort des pauvres

C'est la Mort qui console, hélas! et qui fait vivre;
C'est le but de la vie, et c'est le seul espoir
Qui, comme un élixir, nous monte et nous enivre,
Et nous donne le cœur de marcher jusqu'au soir;

A travers la tempête, et la neige, et le givre,
C'est la clarté vibrante à notre horizon noir;
C'est l'auberge fameuse inscrite sur le livre,
Où l'on pourra manger, et dormir, et s'asseoir;

C'est un Ange qui tient dans ses doigts magnétiques
Le sommeil et le don des rêves extatiques,
Et qui refait le lit des gens pauvres et nus;

C'est la gloire des Dieux, c'est le grenier mystique,
C'est la bourse du pauvre et sa patrie antique,
C'est le portique ouvert sur les Cieux inconnus!

Charles Baudelaire

Death of the Poor

It is Death which consoles us, alas, and sustains!
It's the goal of life, and the one great hope
That like an elixir, befuddles and cheers,
And gives us the heart to plod on until eve;

Through storm, snow and frost, it's the twinkling light
On our pitch-black horizon gleaming afar;
It's the famous old inn inscribed in the book,
Where one day we shall eat, and shall slumber and rest;

It's an Angel who holds in his magnetic hands
Precious sleep and the blessing of rapturous dreams,
And who remakes the bed of the naked and poor.

It's the glory of Gods, it's the mystical store,
It's the poor man's purse and his ancient home;
It's the portal of Paradise opening wide!

Charles Baudelaire

La Mort des artistes

Combien faut-il de fois secouer mes grelots
Et baiser ton front bas, morne caricature?
Pour piquer dans le but, de mystique nature,
Combien, ô mon carquois, perdre de javelots?

Nous userons notre âme en de subtils complots,
Et nous démolirons mainte lourde armature,
Avant de contempler la grande Créature
Dont l'infernal désir nous remplit de sanglots!

Il en est qui jamais n'ont connu leur Idole,
Et ces sculpteurs damnés et marqués d'un affront,
Qui vont se martelant la poitrine et le front,

N'ont qu'un espoir, étrange et sombre Capitole!
C'est que la Mort, planant comme un soleil nouveau,
Fera s'épanouir les fleurs de leur cerveau!

Death of Artists

How many times must I shake my bells
And kiss thy low brow, dismal caricature?
How many shafts, O my quiver, be lost
Ere I hit the impalpable, mystical mark?

We shall wear out our soul with cunning designs
And demolish many an awkward frame
Before we behold the great Creature for whom
The infernal desire fills our bosom with sobs!

There are some who never their Idol have known,
And these sculptors, condemned and branded with shame,
Who keep beating and hammering breast and brow,

Have only one hope, one strange, dark Capitol!
'Tis that Death, like a new sun afloat in the sky,
Will cause the flowers of their brain to bloom!

Charles Baudelaire

Le Rêve d'un curieux

Connais-tu, comme moi, la douleur savoureuse,
Et de toi fais-tu dire: "Oh! l'homme singulier!"
—J'allais mourir. C'était dans mon âme amoureuse,
Désir mêlé d'horreur, un mal particulier;

Angoisse et vif espoir, sans humeur factieuse.
Plus allait se vidant le fatal sablier,
Plus ma torture était âpre et délicieuse;
Tout mon cœur s'arrachait au monde familier.

J'étais comme l'enfant avide du spectacle,
Haïssant le rideau comme on hait un obstacle . . .
Enfin la vérité froide se révéla:

J'étais mort sans surprise, et la terrible aurore
M'enveloppait. —Eh quoi! n'est-ce donc que cela?
La toile était levée et j'attendais encore.

A Queer Fellow's Dream

Have you known, as have I, voluptuous pain,
And of you do they say: "Oh, what a queer man!"?
—I was dying. My soul brimmed with eager desire
Intermingled with horror, a trouble most strange;

Agony and bright hope, without anger or spite.
The more nearly empty the fatal hour-glass,
The keener my torture and rapture became;
My whole heart was torn out of the world that I knew.

Like the child who can't wait for the show to begin,
I was hating the curtain for blocking the way . . .
At last the cold truth became clearly revealed:

I had died unawares, and the terrible dawn
Had enveloped me. —What! Is this, then, all it is?
The curtain was up, and I waited still.

Charles Baudelaire

Le Voyage

I

Pour l'enfant, amoureux de cartes et d'estampes,
L'univers est égal à son vaste appétit.
Ah! que le monde est grand à la clarté des lampes!
Aux yeux du souvenir que le monde est petit!

Un matin nous partons, le cerveau plein de flamme,
Le cœur gros de rancune et de désirs amers,
Et nous allons, suivant le rhythme de la lame,
Berçant notre infini sur le fini des mers.

Les uns, joyeux de fuir une patrie infâme;
D'autres, l'horreur de leurs berceaux, et quelques-uns,
Astrologues noyés dans les yeux d'une femme,
La Circé tyrannique aux dangereux parfums.

Pour n'être pas changés en bêtes, ils s'enivrent
D'espace et de lumière et de cieux embrasés;
La glace qui les mord, les soleils qui les cuivrent,
Effacent lentement la marque des baisers.

Mais les vrais voyageurs sont ceux-là qui partent
Pour partir; cœurs légers, semblables aux ballons,
De leur fatalité jamais ils ne s'écartent,
Et, sans savoir pourquoi, disent toujours: Allons!

Ceux-là dont les désirs ont la forme des nues,
Et qui rêvent, ainsi qu'un conscrit le canon,
De vastes voluptés, changeantes, inconnues,
Et dont l'esprit humain n'a jamais su le nom!

Travel

I

For the child, fascinated by pictures and maps,
The universe matches his vast appetite.
Ah, how big the world is by the light of the lamps!
By the hindsight of memory, how very small!

We sail off one morning, with brain full of fire,
Heart heavy with rancor and bitter desire,
And we rock, to the rhythmical beat of the waves,
Our infinite soul on the seas' finite breast.

Some are glad to be leaving an odious land,
Some the harsh scene of childhood—and others, a few,
Who are star-gazers drowned in the eyes of a maid,
The tyrannic Circé with her parlous perfumes.

Not to be changed to beasts, these get drunk—not on wine,
But on light and great distance and tropical skies;
The sea-wind's icy bite and the coppering sun
Will efface by degrees the deep brand of the kiss.

But the only true travelers are those who depart
For the sake of departing; hearts light as balloons,
When they're destined to travel they never demur,
But without knowing why, always say: "Let's away!"

They're the ones whose desires have shapes like the clouds
And who dream, as the new conscript dreams of the gun,
Of tremendous delights, ever-changing and strange,
And of which human minds know not even the name!

II

Nous imitons, horreur! la toupie et la boule
Dans leur valse et leurs bonds; même dans nos sommeils
La Curiosité nous tourmente et nous roule,
Comme un Ange cruel qui fouette des soleils.

Singulière fortune où le but se déplace,
Et, n'étant nulle part, peut être n'importe où!
Où l'Homme, dont jamais l'espérance n'est lasse,
Pour trouver le repos court toujours comme un fou!

Notre âme est un trois-mâts cherchant son Icarie;
Une voix retentit sur le pont: "Ouvre l'œil!"
Une voix de la hune, ardente et folle, crie:
"Amour . . . gloire . . . bonheur!" Enfer! c'est un écueil!

Chaque îlot signalé par l'homme de vigie
Est un Eldorado promis par le Destin;
L'Imagination qui dresse son orgie
Ne trouve qu'un récif aux clartés du matin.

O le pauvre amoureux des pays chimériques!
Faut-il le mettre aux fers, le jeter à la mer,
Ce matelot ivrogne, inventeur d'Amériques
Dont le mirage rend le gouffre plus amer?

Tel le vieux vagabond, piétinant dans la boue,
Rêve, le nez en l'air, de brillants paradis;
Son œil ensorcelé découvre une Capoue
Partout où la chandelle illumine un taudis.

II

We behave—horrid thought!—like the top and the ball,
Gyrating and bouncing; even when we're asleep,
Curiosity plagues us and rolls us about,
Like a merciless Angel chastising some suns.

What a strange way to live, when mercurial goals
Are established nowhere, and may be anywhere!
A life in which Man, in whom hope never flags,
Keeps on running like mad—in his search for repose!

Our soul's a three-master, Ikaria-bound;
A voice on the quarterdeck cries: "Look alive!"
A voice from the crow's-nest, impassioned and mad,
Shouts: "Love . . . glory . . . happiness!" Hell! It's a shoal!

Every island the lookout descries and reports
Is an Eldorado that's been promised by Fate;
The Fancy, constructing its orgy to come,
In the clear light of morning finds only a reef.

O the wretched admirer of fanciful lands!
Should we put him in irons, cast him into the sea,
This drunken seafarer, inventing New Worlds,
Whose mirage makes more bitter the briniest deep?

So the old vagabond, as he tramps through the mire,
With his head in the clouds, dreams of bright paradise;
His eye, being spellbound, sees Capua there
Wherever his candle illumines a shack.

III

Etonnants voyageurs! quelles nobles histoires
Nous lisons dans vos yeux profonds comme les mers!
Montrez-nous les écrins de vos riches mémoires,
Ces bijoux merveilleux, faits d'astres et d'éthers.

Nous voulons voyager sans vapeur et sans voile!
Faites, pour égayer l'ennui de nos prisons,
Passer sur nos esprits, tendus comme une toile,
Vos souvenirs avec leurs cadres d'horizons.

Dites, qu'avez-vous vu?

IV

                    "Nous avons vu des astres
Et des flots; nous avons vu des sables aussi;
Et, malgré bien des chocs et d'imprévus désastres,
Nous nous sommes souvent ennuyés, comme ici.

La gloire du soleil sur la mer violette,
La gloire des cités dans le soleil couchant,
Allumaient dans nos cœurs une ardeur inquiète
De plonger dans un ciel au reflet alléchant.

Les plus riches cités, les plus grands paysages,
Jamais ne contenaient l'attrait mystérieux
De ceux que le hasard fait avec les nuages.
Et toujours le désir nous rendait soucieux!

—La jouissance ajoute au désir de la force.
Désir, vieil arbre à qui le plaisir sert d'engrais,
Cependant que grossit et durcit ton écorce,
Tes branches veulent voir le soleil de plus près!

III

Astonishing travelers! What grand, noble tales
We can read in your eyes, which are deep as the seas!
So show us the treasures your memories hold—
Those marvelous gems, wrought of ethers and stars.

We also would travel—without steam or sail!
To enliven our prison's dull boredom, transfer
To our minds, tightly stretched like a canvas, the scenes
You remember, complete with horizons for frames.

Tell us, what did you see?

IV

       "We saw planets and stars;
We saw billows and breakers, and beaches of sand;
And despite many shocks and calamities dire,
We often felt bored, as we used to do here.

The splendor of sunlight on violet seas,
The splendor of cities at sunset aglow,
Would arouse in our hearts a great yearning to plunge
Into some lovely sky whose reflection allured.

The richest of cities, the greatest landscapes
Would for us never hold the mysterious charm
Of the ones that pure chance makes appear in the clouds.
And we still felt the keen, anxious pangs of desire!

—Enjoyment just adds greater strength to desire.
O Desire, thou old tree pleasure serves to manure,
While thy bark, as time passes, becomes thick and tough,
Thy branches reach high, for close view of the sun!

Grandiras-tu toujours, grand arbre plus vivace
Que le cyprès? —Pourtant nous avons, avec soin,
Cueilli quelques croquis pour votre album vorace,
Frères qui trouvez beau tout ce qui vient de loin!

Nous avons salué des idoles à trompe;
Des trônes constellés de joyaux lumineux;
Des palais ouvragés dont la féerique pompe
Serait pour vos banquiers un rêve ruineux;

Des costumes qui sont pour les yeux une ivresse;
Des femmes dont les dents et les ongles sont teints,
Et des jongleurs savants que le serpent caresse."

V

Et puis, et puis encore?

VI

"O cerveaux enfantins!

Pour ne pas oublier la chose capitale,
Nous avons vu partout, et sans l'avoir cherché,
Du haut jusques en bas de l'échelle fatale,
Le spectacle ennuyeux de l'immortel péché:

La femme, esclave vile, orgueilleuse et stupide,
Sans rire s'adorant et s'aimant sans dégoût;
L'homme, tyran goulu, paillard, dur et cupide,
Esclave de l'esclave et ruisseau dans l'égout;

Wilt thou never stop growing, great tree more long-lived
Than the cypress? —We did, though, collect with great care
A few sketches your voracious album to fill,
You admirers of everything come from afar!

We kowtowed to idols with trunks; we beheld
Rich thrones constellated with luminous gems;
Elaborate palaces, fairy-tale pomp
That would be for your bankers a ruinous dream;

Costumes a ravishing feast for the eyes;
Women who've tinted their teeth and their nails,
And masterful jugglers by serpents caressed."

V

And what then? And what else?

VI

"O childish minds!

Yes, we must not forget the one capital thing;
We saw everywhere, and without having sought,
From the top to the bottom of destiny's scale,
The dull, boring pageant of immortal sin;

Woman a vile slave, empty-headed and vain,
Sans humor or nausea adoring herself;
Man a gluttonous tyrant, harsh, greedy and lewd,
The slave's slave and foul path to the gutter or worse;

Le bourreau qui jouit, le martyr qui sanglote;
La fête qu'assaisonne et parfume le sang;
Le poison du pouvoir énervant le despote,
Et le peuple amoureux du fouet abrutissant;

Plusieurs religions semblables à la nôtre,
Toutes escaladant le ciel; la Sainteté,
Comme en un lit de plume un délicat se vautre,
Dans les clous et le crin cherchant la volupté;

L'Humanité bavarde, ivre de son génie,
Et folle, maintenant comme elle était jadis,
Criant à Dieu, dans sa furibonde agonie:
"O mon semblable, ô mon maître, je te maudis!"

Et les moins sots, hardis amants de la Démence,
Fuyant le grand troupeau parqué par le Destin,
Et se réfugiant dans l'opium immense!
—Tel est du globe entier l'éternel bulletin."

VII

Amer savoir, celui qu'on tire du voyage!
Le monde, monotone et petit, aujourd'hui,
Hier, demain, toujours, nous fait voir notre image:
Une oasis d'horreur dans un désert d'ennui!

Faut-il partir? rester? Si tu peux rester, reste;
Pars, s'il le faut. L'un court, et l'autre se tapit
Pour tromper l'ennemi vigilant et funeste,
Le Temps! Il est, hélas! des coureurs sans répit,

Comme le Juif errant et comme les apôtres,
A qui rien ne suffit, ni wagon ni vaisseau,

The hangman's enjoyment, the martyr's great sobs,
The festival seasoned and scented with blood;
The poison of power sapping despots of strength,
And the people grown fond of the whip's cruel lash;

Half a dozen religions resembling our own,
All ascendant to Heaven; the Holy Elite,
Like a fop wallowing in a soft feather-bed,
Seeking pleasure in badges of rank and brocade;

Mankind garrulous, glib, with its genius drunk,
And mad, as mad now as it always has been,
In its furious agony crying to God:
'O my image, my master, I call thee accursed!'

And the least stupid, daring Dementia to court,
Escaping the great herd impounded by Fate,
And taking their refuge in opium's cloud!
—That's the word for all time, from all over the globe."

VII

Bitter knowledge, that which one from travel derives!
The world, small and tiresome, today, yesterday,
Tomorrow, always, just reflects what we are:
An oasis of filth in a desert ennui!

Should one go, or remain? Stay at home if you can;
Depart if you must. Some will run, others hide,
To defraud the dread foe, ever-vigilant Time!
There are some, alas, runners who never can rest,

Like the Wandering Jew and apostles, for whom
Naught suffices, no vessel, no train, to escape

Pour fuir ce rétiaire infâme; il en est d'autres
Qui savent le tuer sans quitter leur berceau.

Lorsque enfin il mettra le pied sur notre échine,
Nous pourrons espérer et crier: En avant!
De même qu'autrefois nous partions pour la Chine,
Les yeux fixés au large et les cheveux au vent.

Nous nous embarquerons sur la mer des Ténèbres
Avec le cœur joyeux d'un jeune passager.
Entendez-vous ces voix, charmantes et funèbres,
Qui chantent: "Par ici! vous qui voulez manger

Le Lotus parfumé! c'est ici qu'on vendange
Les fruits miraculeux dont votre cœur a faim;
Venez vous enivrer de la douceur étrange
De cette après-midi qui n'a jamais de fin!"

A l'accent familier nous devinons le spectre;
Nos Pylades là-bas tendent leurs bras vers nous.
"Pour rafraîchir ton cœur nage vers ton Electre!"
Dit celle dont jadis nous baisions les genoux.

VIII

O Mort, vieux capitaine, il est temps! levons l'ancre!
Ce pays nous ennuie, ô Mort! Appareillons!
Si le ciel et la mer sont noirs comme de l'encre,
Nos cœurs que tu connais sont remplis de rayons!

Verse-nous ton poison pour qu'il nous réconforte!
Nous voulons, tant ce feu nous brûle le cerveau,
Plonger au fond du gouffre, Enfer ou Ciel, qu'importe?
Au fond de l'Inconnu pour trouver du *nouveau*!

From that infamous web-thrower; others there are
Who can kill him without ever leaving their crib.

When he finally does plant his foot on our spine,
We can hope and cry: "Forward! Onward! Away!"
Just as in the old days we would sail for Cathay
With our eyes fixed to seaward and hair to the wind.

On the Ocean of Darkness we'll gaily embark
With the gladness of heart of a passenger youth.
Do you hear them, those voices, enticing, deep-toned,
That keep chanting: "This way, you who long to partake

Of the sweet-scented Lotus! It's harvested here,
That miraculous fruit that your heart hungers for;
Come and put yourself under the strange, drunken spell
Of this long afternoon stretching on without end!"

The accent's familiar—we divine who it is;
Our Pylades over there hold their arms out to us.
"Swim toward your Electra, refreshen your heart!"
Says that woman whose knees long ago we would kiss.

VIII

O Death, old sea-captain, it's time! Let's weigh anchor!
We fret at this sojourn, O Death! Let's set sail!
Though the sky and the sea be as dark as black ink,
Our hearts, as you know, are aglow with bright rays!

So pour us your lethal, all-comforting draft!
Our brains are on fire; we are eager to plunge
Deep into the abyss—Hell or Heaven, what odds?
Deep into the Unknown, just to find something new!

Charles Baudelaire

Le Coucher du soleil romantique

Que le soleil est beau quand tout frais il se lève,
Comme une explosion nous lançant son bonjour!
—Bienheureux celui-là qui peut avec amour
Saluer son coucher plus glorieux qu'un rêve!

Je me souviens! . . . J'ai vu tout, fleur, source, sillon,
Se pâmer sous son œil comme un cœur qui palpite . . .
—Courons vers l'horizon, il est tard, courons vite,
Pour attraper au moins un oblique rayon!

Mais je poursuis en vain le Dieu qui se retire;
L'irrésistible Nuit établit son empire,
Noire, humide, funeste et pleine de frissons;

Une odeur de tombeau dans les ténèbres nage,
Et mon pied peureux froisse, au bord du marécage,
Des crapauds imprévus et de froids limaçons.

Romantic Sunset

How fine is the sun when he rises afresh
Like a great burst of fireworks to bid us good day!
—Thrice blest whosoever can lovingly hail
His setting, resplendent beyond any dream!

I remember! . . . how furrow, flower and rill
All basked in his glance like a beating heart . . .
—Let's run westward, and quickly, before it's too late,
To catch at least one of his last oblique rays!

But in vain I pursue the withdrawing God;
Irresistible Night has established her sway,
Dark, humid and baneful, all shudders and dread;

In the darkness there floats a whiff of the grave,
And my fearful foot treads, at the brink of the fen,
On startling toads and on cold, clammy snails.

Charles Baudelaire

A une Malabaraise

Tes pieds sont aussi fins que tes mains et ta hanche
Est large à faire envie à la plus belle blanche;
A l'artiste pensif ton corps est doux et cher;
Tes grands yeux de velours sont plus noirs que ta chair.
Aux pays chauds et bleus où ton Dieu t'a fait naître,
Ta tâche est d'allumer la pipe de ton maître,
De pourvoir les flacons d'eau fraîches et d'odeurs,
De chasser loin du lit les moustiques rôdeurs,
Et, dès que le matin fait chanter les platanes,
D'acheter au bazar ananas et bananes.
Tout le jour, où tu veux, tu mènes tes pieds nus,
Et fredonnes tout bas de vieux airs inconnus;
Et quand descend le soir au manteau d'écarlate,
Tu poses doucement ton corps sur une natte,
Où tes rêves flottants sont pleins de colibris,
Et toujours, comme toi, gracieux et fleuris.

Pourquoi, l'heureuse enfant, veux-tu voir notre France,
Ce pays trop peuplé que fauche la souffrance,
Et, confiant ta vie aux bras forts des marins,
Faire de grands adieux à tes chers tamarins?
Toi, vêtue à moitié de mousselines frêles,
Frissonnante là-bas sous la neige et les grêles,
Comme tu pleurerais tes loisirs doux et francs,
Si, le corset brutal emprisonnant tes flancs,
Il te fallait glaner ton souper dans nos fanges
Et vendre le parfum de tes charmes étranges,
L'œil pensif, et suivant, dans nos sales brouillards,
Des cocotiers absents les fantômes épars!

Charles Baudelaire

To a Malabar Girl

Your small feet are as fine as your hands, and your hips
Broad enough to make envious any white belle;
Your form, to an artist, is priceless and sweet;
Your great velvet eyes darker brown than your skin.
In the warm, sunny land where your God gave you life,
Your tasks are to kindle your master's filled pipe,
To replenish the jars with fresh water and scent,
To chase roving mosquitoes away from the beds,
And when morning winds cause the plane-trees to sing,
To buy mangoes and pineapples in the bazaar.
All day long you go, barefoot, wherever you like,
Contentedly humming your curious old tunes;
And when night with its mantle of scarlet descends,
You dispose yourself quietly on a straw mat,
Where your untroubled dreams are of bright humming-birds,
And like you, always dainty and flower-bedecked.

Oh why, happy child, should you crave to see France,
That too-populous country where suffering's rife,
And, entrusting your life to the sailors' strong arms,
Bid reluctant farewell to your dear marmosets?
Semi-clad as you are in a thin muslin dress,
Shivering over there in the snow and the hail,
How you'd weep for your free, pleasant, leisurely life
If, with brutal tight corset confining your flanks,
You were forced to subsist on our refuse and vice,
And to sell the exotic bouquet of your charms,
Nostalgically seeking, in our wretched fogs,
The sparse apparitions of faraway palms!

Charles Baudelaire

*   *   *

N'est-ce pas qu'il est doux, maintenant que nous sommes
Fatigués et flétris comme les autres hommes,
De chercher quelquefois à l'Orient lointain
Si nous voyons encor les rougeurs du matin,
Et, quand nous avançons dans la rude carrière,
D'écouter les échos qui chantent en arrière
Et les chuchotements de ces jeunes amours
Que le Seigneur a mis au début de nos jours?

Retrospect

Is it not sweet for us, now that we have become
Fatigued and wilted by the years like other men,
To look back now and then toward the distant East
For what we still can see of morning's rosy glow,
And, when we're far advanced along the rugged path,
To hearken to the echoes drifting back to us,
And to the whisperings of those young love affairs
The Lord vouchsafed to grant us early in our days?

Charles Baudelaire

Hymne

A la très-chère, à la très-belle
Qui remplit mon cœur de clarté,
A l'ange, à l'idole immortelle,
Salut en immortalité!

Elle se répand dans ma vie
Comme un air imprégné de sel,
Et dans mon âme inassouvie
Verse le goût de l'éternel.

Sachet toujours frais qui parfume
L'atmosphère d'un cher réduit,
Encensoir oublié qui fume
En secret à travers la nuit,

Comment, amour incorruptible,
T'exprimer avec vérité?
Grain de musc qui gis, invisible,
Au fond de mon éternité!

A la très-bonne, à la très-belle
Qui fait ma joie et ma santé,
A l'ange, à l'idole immortelle,
Salut en immortalité!

Hymn

To her most dear, to her most fair
Who fills my heart with radiant light,
Immortal idol, angel bright,
All hail, forever and a day!

She permeates through all my life
Like air impregnated with salt,
And into my unsated soul
The taste of the eternal pours.

Still-fresh sachet that keeps perfumed
The air of a beloved retreat,
Forgotten censer left to smoke
In secret on throughout the night,

Love incorruptible—how to
Express most truly what you are?
A grain of musk, you lie unseen
Deep down in my eternal core!

To her most sweet, to her most fair
Who makes my happiness and health,
Immortal idol, angel bright,
All hail, forever and a day!

Le Vase brisé

Le vase où meurt cette verveine
D'un coup d'éventail fut fêlé;
Le coup dut l'effleurer à peine,
Aucun bruit ne l'a révélé.

Mais la légère meurtrissure,
Mordant le cristal chaque jour,
D'une marche invisible et sûre
En a fait lentement le tour.

Son eau fraîche a fui goutte à goutte,
Le suc des fleurs s'est épuisé;
Personne encore ne s'en doute:
N'y touchez pas, il est brisé.

Souvent aussi la main qu'on aime,
Effleurant le coeur, le meurtrit;
Puis le coeur se fend de lui-même,
La fleur de son amour périt.

Toujours intact aux yeux du monde,
Il sent croître et pleurer tout bas
Sa blessure fine et profonde:
Il est brisé, n'y touchez pas.

Armand Sully Prudhomme

The Broken Vase

That vase where my verbena dies
Was cracked by some fair lady's fan.
It must have been the merest touch;
No sound it made gave it away.

But that crack, so minute at first,
By eating daily into glass,
Has surely and invisibly
Crept all the way around the vase.

Its water's leaked out drop by drop;
The flowers' sap has ebbed away.
No one as yet suspects the truth:
The vase is broken; touch it not.

Just so, ofttimes, the hand one loves
Will bruise one's heart, and leave it sore.
The heart then of itself will break;
Its bloom of love will wilt and die.

Still quite intact to others' eyes,
It feels its wound severe and deep
Grow ever larger, ooze and weep:
The heart is broken; touch it not.

Le Rendez-vous

Il est tard. L'astronome aux veilles obstinées,
Sur sa tour, dans le ciel où meurt le dernier bruit,
Cherche des îles d'or, et le front dans la nuit,
Regarde à l'infini blanchir des matinées;

Les mondes fuient pareils à des graines vannées;
L'épais fourmillement des nébuleuses luit;
Mais, attentif à l'astre échevelé qu'il suit,
Il le somme et lui dit: "Reviens dans mille années."

Et l'astre reviendra. D'un pas ni d'un instant
Il ne saurait frauder la science éternelle;
Des hommes passeront, l'humanité l'attend;

D'un oeil changeant, mais sûr, elle fait sentinelle;
Et, fût-elle abolie au temps de son retour,
Seule, la Vérité veillerait sur la tour.

The Rendezvous

It's late. The dogged, vigilant astronomer,
Upon his tower, scans the boundless, soundless sky
For golden isles of light, his brow in darkest night,
And watches countless dawns illume the infinite.

The spinning planets fall away like winnowed grain;
The thickly swarming nebulae are all aglow;
But he, intent upon one odd, disheveled star,
Commands it: "Come you back, one thousand years from now!"

And that star will come back. Not by one instant nor
One step could it defraud eternal Nature's law.
Some men will pass; humanity will still await.

With changing eye, but sure, it stands as sentinel;
And should mankind have perished when that star returns,
Then Truth herself would watch, alone upon the tower.

Les Yeux

Bleus ou noirs, tous aimés, tous beaux,
Des yeux sans nombre ont vu l'aurore;
Ils dorment au fond des tombeaux,
Et le soleil se lève encore.

Les nuits, plus douces que les jours,
Ont enchanté des yeux sans nombre;
Les étoiles brillent toujours,
Et les yeux se sont remplis d'ombre.

O! qu'ils aient perdu le regard,
Non, non, cela n'est pas possible!
Ils se sont tournées quelque part,
Vers ce qu'on nomme l'invisible;

Et comme les astres penchants
Nous quittent, mais au ciel demeurent,
Les prunelles ont leurs couchants,
Mais il n'est pas vrai qu'elles meurent.

Bleus ou noirs, tous aimés, tous beaux,
Ouverts à quelque immense aurore,
De l'autre côté des tombeaux,
Les yeux qu'on ferme voient encore.

Eyes

Blue, grey or dark, all loved, all fair,
Eyes numberless have seen the dawn.
Now closed, they sleep down in their graves;
And morning sunrise still goes on.

Night skies, more tranquil than the day's,
Have fascinated countless eyes.
The stars of night still scintillate;
And pitchy dark has filled the eyes.

But—have they lost their power of sight?
No, no! That is not possible!
They must have turned to look somewhere
At what we call invisible.

As setting stars take leave of us
But keep their places in the sky,
Eye-pupils wane like setting suns,
But 'tis not true they really die.

Blue, grey or dark, all loved, all fair,
Reopened to some great new dawn
Which breaks for them beyond the grave,
The eyes we close see on and on.

Les Conquérants

Comme un vol de gerfauts hors du charnier natal,
Fatigués de porter leurs misères hautaines,
De Palos de Moguer routiers et capitaines
Partaient, ivres d'un rêve héroïque et brutal.

Ils allaient conquérir le fabuleux métal
Que Cipango mûrit dans ses mines lointaines,
Et les vents alizés inclinaient leurs antennes
Aux bords mystérieux du monde occidental.

Chaque soir, espérant des lendemains épiques,
L'azur phosphorescent de la mer des Tropiques
Enchantait leur sommeil d'un mirage doré;

Ou, penchés à l'avant des blanches caravelles,
Ils regardaient monter en un ciel ignoré
Du fond de l'Océan des étoiles nouvelles.

The Conquerors

Like a flight of gyrfalcons from one lofty nest,
Tired of squalor and bones they no longer could bear,
Out from Palos of Spain sailed in ship after ship
Men and captains, all drunk on a bold, brutal dream.

They were going to vanquish the fabulous gold
That Cipango* secretes in her faraway mines,
And the easterly trade-winds inclined their lateens
To mysterious shores of the new western world.

They would savor each night epic days soon to come,
And the phosphorous blue of the Tropical sea
Would enrapture their sleep with a golden mirage;

Or, hunched over the bow of their white caravels,
They would watch as new stars, rising out of the sea
On the southern horizon, their firmament changed.

* Cipango: Marco Polo's word for Japan.

José-Maria de Heredia

Jouvence

Juan Ponce de Leon, par le Diable tenté,
Déjà très vieux et plein des antiques études,
Voyant l'âge blanchir ses cheveux courts et rudes,
Prit la mer pour chercher la Source de Santé.

Sur sa belle Armada, d'un vain songe hanté,
Trois ans il explora les glauques solitudes,
Lorsque enfin, déchirant le brouillard des Bermudes,
La Floride apparut sous un ciel enchanté.

Et le Conquistador, bénissant sa folie,
Vint planter son pennon d'une main affaiblie
Dans la terre éclatante où s'ouvrait son tombeau.

Vieillard, tu fus heureux et ta fortune est telle
Que la Mort, malgré toi, fit ton rêve plus beau;
La Gloire t'a donné la Jeunesse immortelle.

Youth

Juan Ponce de Leon, by Satan sorely tried,
Well on in years, and steeped in ancient classic lore,
On seeing age turn white his short, unruly hair,
Sailed off to seek the Source, the Fountainhead of Youth.

Aboard his handsome Fleet, obsessed by that vain dream,
He spent three years exploring glaucous empty seas;
Then finally, out from behind Bermuda's mists,
His Florida appeared, beneath enchanted skies.

And the Conquistador, his madness having blest,
Debarked to plant his pennon with a feeble hand
Upon the dazzling land where soon would yawn his tomb.

Old man, you had good luck—indeed, so very good
That Death, in spite of you, embellished your great dream;
For Fame has given you an everlasting Youth.

José-Maria de Heredia

Le Tombeau du Conquérant

A l'ombre de la voûte en fleur des catalpas
Et des tulipiers noirs qu'étoile un blanc pétale,
Il ne repose point dans la terre fatale;
La Floride conquise a manqué sous ses pas.

Un vil tombeau messied à de pareils trépas.
Linceul du Conquérant de L'Inde Occidentale,
Tout le Meschacébé par-dessus lui s'étale.
Le Peau Rouge et l'ours gris ne le troubleront pas.

Il dort au lit profond creusé par les eaux vierges.
Qu'importe un monument funéraire, des cierges,
Le psaume et la chapelle ardente et l'ex-voto?

Puisque le vent du Nord, parmi les cyprières,
Pleure et chante à jamais d'éternelles prières
Sur le Grand Fleuve où gît Hernando de Soto.

The Tomb of the Conqueror

In the shade of high-vaulted catalpas in bloom
And dark tulip-trees spangled with blossoms of white
He reposes, but not in earth's fated embrace;
Florida proved too small for his conquering strides.

A mere tomb is unworthy of such noble dead.
For the West Indies' conqueror, water's the shroud;
The whole vast Mississippi is over him spread.
Nary redskin nor grizzly will trouble his rest,

For he sleeps in the primeval waters' deep bed.
Of what moment a tombstone, some candles, the psalm,
The funeral chapel and plaque ex-voto?

The North Wind in the cypresses grieves for his soul
As it chants its eternal orisons above
The Great River where lies Hernando de Soto.

Paris

C'est vrai, j'aime Paris d'une amitié malsaine;
J'ai partout le regret des vieux bords de la Seine.
Devant la vaste mer, devant les pics neigeux,
Je rêve d'un faubourg plein d'enfance et de jeux,
D'un coteau tout pelé où ma Muse s'applique
A noter les tons fins d'un ciel mélancolique,
D'un bout de Bièvre, avec quelques champs oubliés
Où l'on tend une corde aux troncs des peupliers,
Pour y faire sécher la toile et la flanelle,
Ou d'un coin pour pêcher dans l'île de Grenelle.

Paris

It's true, I love Paris with mawkish tenderness.
Go where I may, I miss the old banks of the Seine.
When I'm beside the sea, or viewing snowy peaks,
I dream of neighborhoods where swarms of children play,
Of a bald knoll from which my Muse appreciates
The subtle variegations of a somber sky,
Of Bièvre's shoreline, with some half-forgotten tracts
Where people stretch a cord between scrub-poplar trunks
For hanging flannel clothes and bedding out to dry,
Or of a fishing-hole on the isle of Grenelle.

Translator's Notes:

For rhythm's sake, give "Paris" its French pronunciation in the
opening line.

The Bièvre is a small stream which becomes part of the city's
sewer-drainage system.

François Coppée

La Mort des Oiseaux

Le soir, au coin du feu, j'ai pensé bien des fois
A la mort d'un oiseau, quelque part, dans les bois.
Pendant les tristes jours de l'hiver monotone,
Les pauvres nids déserts, les nids qu'on abandonne,
Se balancent au vent sur le ciel gris de fer.
O! comme les oiseaux doivent mourir l'hiver!
Pourtant, lorsque viendra le temps des violettes,
Nous ne trouverons plus leurs délicats squelettes
Dans le gazon d'avril, où nous irons courir.
Est-ce que les oiseaux se cachent pour mourir?

The Death of Birds

At eve, beside the fire, I've wondered many times
About the way birds die, out somewhere in the wild.
Day after dreary day, in winter's changeless gloom,
The poor deserted nests, the nests they leave behind,
Keep swaying in the wind against the iron-gray sky.
Alas! How many birds must die, when winter reigns!
And yet, when once again it's time for violets,
We'll find no trace of them, no fragile skeletons
Amidst the April grass in which we'll go and run.
Do birds go off and hide, when they're about to die?

Le Somnambule

Le chapeau sur la tête et la canne à la main,
Serrant dans un frac noir sa rigide ossature,
Il allait et venait au bord de la toiture,
D'un air automatique et d'un pas surhumain.

Singulier promeneur, spectre et caricature,
Sans cesse, il refaisait son terrible chemin.
Sur le ciel orageux, couleur de parchemin,
Il dessinait sa haute et funèbre stature.

Soudain, à la lueur d'un éclair infernal,
Comme il frisait le vide en rasant le chenal
Avec le pied danseur et vif d'un funambule,

L'horreur emplit mon être et figea tout mon sang,
Car un grand chat d'ébène hydrophobe et grincant
Venait de réveiller le monsieur somnambule.

The Sleep-Walker

With his hat on his head and his cane in his hand,
A black morning-coat hugging his stiff, bony frame,
He stepped this way and that on the edge of the roof
Like an automaton, superhumanly spry.

A singular stroller, ghost, caricature,
He kept walking, retracing his perilous path.
On a parchment-hued background of threatening sky,
His funereal figure loomed tall and clear-cut.

Of a sudden, an infernal lightning-bolt flashed
As he skirted the void, barely missing the drain,
With the quick, dancing step of a funambulist,

And stark horror filled me, congealing my blood,
For an ebony cat hydrophobic and huge
With a screech had just wakened the sleep-walking man.

Le Mauvais oeil

Le mauvais œil me persécute:
Un œil où le blâme reluit,
Où la haine se répercute,
Fixe et vitreux comme celui
Du condamné qu'on exécute.

Sans que jamais il se rebute,
Il me précède ou me poursuit,
Où que j'aille, où que mon pied bute,
     Le mauvais œil!

Et je suis tellement en butte
A cet œil jaune qui me nuit
Que je le vois même la nuit;
Et dompteur dont je suis la brute,
Dans l'ombre il me vrille et me scrute,
     Le mauvais œil!

The Evil Eye

The evil eye's tormenting me:
An eye wherein harsh censure gleams,
Wherein pure hatred fulgurates;
A glassy, staring eye like that
Of one to execution damned.

Without surcease, relentlessly,
It goes before or after me,
No matter where I walk or lurch—
      The evil eye!

So utterly exposed am I
To that malignant yellow eye,
I see it even in the dark:
A tamer whose foiled beast I be,
Transfixing, scrutinizing me—
      The evil eye!

Le Vieux mouton

Trop âgé pour avoir pu suivre le troupeau,
Il était resté là, perdu comme une épave;
Et dans un gouffre, auprès d'un torrent plein de bave,
Il traînait le cancer qui lui mangeait la peau.

Le fait est que le Diable en eût fait un suppôt,
Tant la sorcellerie habitait son œil cave
Et tant il avait pris, sur le bord de ce gave,
La nudité du ver et le pas du crapaud.

Je m'enfuis! Car la bête accueillait mon approche
Avec un bêlement de haine et de reproche
Strident comme une voix qui crie: "A l'assassin!"

Et la nuit ténébreuse installait son royaume,
Que j'entendais toujours sangloter en mon sein
La malédiction du vieux mouton fantôme.

The Old Sheep

Too old to have kept up with the departed flock,
He had remained behind, like jetsam cast aside,
And down a gorge, along a foaming torrent's brim,
He slowly dragged his scabrous, cancer-eaten hide.

Truth is, the Devil might have made a tool of him,
So much did witchcraft lurk within his hollow eye,
And so much did he seem, beside that mountain stream,
As naked as a worm, as graceless as a toad.

I fled! because the beast was greeting my approach
With raucous, frenzied bleats of hatred and reproach,
As strident as a voice exclaiming: "Murder! Help!"

And as the dark of night established its domain,
I still kept hearing sob within me, flouting sleep,
The malediction of the phantomesque old sheep.

L'Etang

Plein de très vieux poissons frappés de cécité,
L'étang, sous un ciel bas roulant de sourds tonnerres,
Etale entre ses joncs plusieurs fois centenaires
La clapotante horreur de son opacité.

Là-bas, des farfadets servent de luminaires
A plus d'un marais noir, sinistre et redouté;
Mais lui ne se révèle en ce lieu déserté
Que par ses bruits affreux de crapauds poitrinaires.

Or, la lune qui point tout juste en ce moment,
Semble s'y regarder si fantastiquement,
Que l'on dirait, à voir sa spectrale figure,

Son nez plat et le vague étrange de ses dents,
Une tête de mort éclairée en dedans
Qui viendrait se mirer dans une glace obscure.

The Mere

Full of decrepit fish, senile and stricken blind,
The mere, beneath low clouds whence hollow thunder rolls,
Displays among its rank antediluvian reeds
The plashing loathsomeness of its opacity.

Down there, wills-o'-the-wisp provide the only light
To more than one forbidding, sinister black bog;
But in that lonely place, these give no telltale sign
Save the macabre croaks of their consumptive frogs.

The moon, which heaves in sight at just this moment, seems
To contemplate its image there so eerily
That one might think, to see its spectral countenance,

Its flattened nose and oddly vague and shapeless teeth,
That it's a dead man's skull illumined from within,
Come to regard itself in a dim looking-glass.

Maurice Rollinat

Le Maniaque

Je frissonne toujours à l'aspect singulier
De certaine bottine ou de certain soulier.
Oui, (que pour me railler vos épaules se haussent!)
Je frissonne: et soudain, songeant au pied qu'ils chaussent,
Je me demande: "Est-il mécanique ou vivant?"
Et je suis pas à pas le sujet, l'observant,
Et cherchant l'appareil d'acier que se dérobe
Sous le pantalon fin ou sous la belle robe,
Et dès qu'il a relui, maniaque aux abois,
Dans le cuir élégant je flaire un pied de bois.

The Maniac

I always have to shudder at the curious sight
Of someone wearing a peculiar boot or shoe.
I shudder, yes (so shrug and mock me if you will),
And of a sudden, thinking of the foot thus shod,
I ask myself: "Mechanical, or flesh and blood?"
I follow closely such a person, keeping watch
To spy the metal apparatus hidden there
Beneath the well-cut trouser-leg or lovely gown;
And when it gleams, then I, a maniac in full cry,
Within the stylish leather ~~scent~~ *smell* a wooden leg.

La Dame en cire

Je regardais tourner le mannequin,
Et j'admirais sa taille, sa poitrine,
Ses cheveux d'or et son minois taquin,
Lorsque j'ai vu palpiter sa narine
Et son cou mince à forme vipérine.
—"Elle vit donc!" me dis-je, épouvanté;
Et depuis lors, à toute heure hanté
Par un amour que rien ne peut occire,
J'ai la peur et la curiosité
De voir entrer chez moi la dame en cire.

Par tous les temps, sous un ciel africain,
Et sous la nue inquiète ou chagrine,
Comme un nageur que poursuit un requin,
Sans pouvoir fuir je reste à sa vitrine,
Et là j'entends mon cœur qui tambourine.
J'ai beau me dire: "Horreur! Insanité!"
Il est des nuits d'affreuse obscurité,
—Tant je l'évoque et tant je la désire!—
Où je conçois la possibilité
De voir entrer chez moi la dame en cire!

Telle qu'elle est, en robe de nankin,
Avec ses yeux couleur d'aigue-marine
Et son sourire attirant et coquin,
La pivoteuse à bouche purpurine
Dans mon cerveau s'installe et se burine.
Je m'hallucine avec avidité
Et je m'enfonce, ivre d'étrangeté,

The Wax Lady

I was watching the mannequin turn
And admiring her figure, her bust,
Her blond hair and her pert little face,
When I noticed a twitch in her nose
And her neck, slim and round like a snake.
"She's alive!" I exclaimed, thunderstruck;
And since then, haunted day and night by
A great passion that nothing can quench,
I've been dreading and craving to see
The wax lady come calling on me.

In all weathers, in African sun,
Under stormy or overcast skies,
Like a swimmer pursued by a shark,
From her window I can't get away,
And I hear my heart drumming all day.
I say: "Fool! You're insane!" —but in vain;
And some nights when it's frightfully dark,
—I conjure and desire her so much!—
I conceive how I might get to see
The wax lady come calling on me!

As she is, in her gown of nankeen,
With her eyes of pale aquamarine
And her mischievous, come-hither smile,
The magenta-mouthed swiveling dame
Is embedded and etched in my brain.
I hallucinate avidly now,
And I sink, drunk on strangeness, into

Dans un brouillard que ma raison déchire,
Car c'est mon rêve ardemment souhaité
De voir entrer chez moi la dame en cire.

Envoi

Ô toi qui m'as si souvent visité,
Satan! vieux roi de la perversité,
Fais-moi la grâce, ô sulfureux Messire,
Par un minuit lugubrement tinté,
De voir entrer chez moi la dame en cire!

A thick fog that my mind tears away,
For my ardent dream-wish is to see
The wax lady come calling on me.

Envoi

You who've so often visited me,
Old King Satan of Perversity,
Please drop in, O sulfurous Messire,
On some midnight's stroke dismal, and see
The wax lady come calling on me!

Le Mime

Par quelle fantaisie insolite et malsaine
En vins-je à grimacer devant ma glace, un soir,
Un soir de fin d'automne où Paris, mome et noir,
Pompait lugubrement les brouillards de la Seine?

Le fait est que mêlant la tendresse à la haine,
Le rage à la stupeur, le rire au désespoir,
Ma physionomie en face du miroir
Passa par tous les tons de la mimique humaine.

Et je me recueillais dans ma sincérité
Pour rendre avec une âpre et stricte vérité
Le rictus d'un démon qui maudit sa science,

Quand je vis dans l'éclair du miroir glauque et nu,
Au lieu de mon visage, un visage inconnu
Où se répercutait ma propre conscience!

The Mime

By what extraordinary, crazy whim did I
Come to grimace one night before my mirror's eye,
One chill late-autumn night when Paris, dark and bleak,
Was glumly sucking up the mists from off the Seine?

The fact is that by mixing tenderness with hate,
Astonishment with rage, and laughter with despair,
My physiognomy, reflected in the glass,
Played every single key of human mimicry;

And as I concentrated with sincerity
On rendering with keenest, strictest verity
The rictus of a demon cursing his black art,

I saw framed in the mirror's glaucous, naked light,
Instead of my own face, a visage strange to me,
Wherein there flashed my own true personality!

Les Becs de gaz

Les becs de gaz des mauvais coins
Eclairent les filous en loques
Et ceux qui, pleins de soliloques,
S'en vont jaunes comme des coings.

Complices des rôdeurs chafouins
Guettant le Monsieur à breloques,
Les becs de gaz des mauvais coins
Eclairent les filous en loques.

Et coups de couteau, coups de poings,
Coups de sifflets, cris équivoques,
Spectres hideux, mouchards baroques,
Tout ce mystère a pour témoins
Les becs de gaz des mauvais coins.

Gas-Lamps

Gas-lamps on streets of ill repute
Illuminate for ragged rogues
And those, full of soliloquies,
Who sail with three sheets to the wind.

Accomplices of prowlers sly
Who stalk the dude with silver fobs,
Gas-lamps on streets of ill repute
Illuminate for ragged rogues.

And knifings, beatings, fisticuffs,
Shrill whistles, muffled cries and shouts,
Stool pigeons, horrid spooks—all such
Mysterious stuff is witnessed by
Gas-lamps on streets of ill repute.

AFTERWORD ON RHYTHM

For any would-be translator of poetry, the achievement of substantial similarity of rhythm between foreign original and English version is a special problem; for the sound systems and rhythm patterns of other languages differ in various respects from those of English.

In French poetry, for instance, the very existence of *meter* is categorically denied. Instead of hearkening to the patter of little metric feet, the French insist that no single syllable of any poetic line should be stressed appreciably, except the last one. In their view the whole line, regardless of its length, is the only rhythmic unit. This means that all a French poet really has to do, insofar as rhythm is concerned, is to make sure he has the right number of syllables (including "mute *e*" syllables) in each poetic line.

Consequently, in trying to emulate the rhythmic effect of a French poem, I find syllable-counting to be a very useful technique. Keeping the French syllable-count constantly in mind, I strive to make each line of my English translation match its French counterpart in number of syllables. When a perfect or near-perfect match has been achieved for every line of a poem, I feel that this establishes an authenticated "infrastructure" for the overall rhythm of that poem in English.

Such an infrastructure then makes it relatively easy for me to come up with a suitable metric pattern, to enhance my translated version.

K. L.

TRIVIA CONCERNING THE POETS
TRANSLATED

The language of French poets of the 15th and 16th centuries, such as Orléans, Villon, DuBellay and Ronsard, is of course Old French. Although the spelling and syntax of this language are often disconcerting to a modern reader, it is still not as far removed from modern French as is the English of Chaucer and Shakespeare from modern English.

Charles, Duke of Orléans, a French prince of royal blood, was captured by the English in the battle of Agincourt (1415) and spent many years in England as a prisoner. His son became King Louis XII of France.

François Villon, author of the famous line, "Où sont les neiges d'antan?", was a confessed vagabond and rogue. After having killed a man in Paris in 1455, he was incarcerated and eventually was banished from that city for ten years. "Ballad of the Hanged" was evidently written while he was in prison, expecting the capital punishment.

Joachim DuBellay served for several years in the papal state of Rome as secretary to his cousin, Cardinal DuBellay. A member of the Pléiade (a group of contemporary poets), he advocated emulation of the classics and the use of French as the language of literature. "Nostalgia" and "Sonnet for My Barber" illumine some aspects of his life as an expatriate Frenchman in 16th-century Rome.

Pierre de Ronsard, another poet of the Pléiade, penned several volumes of excellent poetry, each book being dedicated to a different lady. As the poems translated here illustrate, the predominant theme of his work is unrequited love. From such evidence, one might very well deduce that members of the fair sex often found his person less charming than his verses.

Jean de La Fontaine is the acknowledged master of the animal fable, commenting with whimsical irony on the behavior of humans. Today the vocabulary of virtually every living language includes some expression equivalent to "sour grapes."

Voltaire (born François-Marie Arouet) is much more celebrated as a philosopher than as a poet. His was one of the strongest voices in the anticlerical "enlightenment" of the 18th century, which laid the groundwork for the French Revolution. His matter-of-fact "Farewell to Life" is typical of his agnosticism.

Marie-Joseph Chénier, brother of the more famous André Chénier, authored a history of French literature and was a member of several important political bodies during the French Revolution, including the Convention, the Council of Five Hundred and the Tribunate.

Alfonse de Lamartine was a very popular Romantic poet whose literary success led him into a political career. For a short time following the Revolution of 1848, he headed the provisional government, but eventually lost out to Louis Napoléon Buonaparte (later Napoleon III of the Second Empire).

Victor Hugo, a true superstar of French letters, was preeminent in the Romantic movement as novelist (*Les Misérables, Notre-Dame de Paris*, etc.), playwright (*Hernani*) and poet. His poetry is rich in variety of subject matter and tone: it can be sensually lyrical ("June Nights"), devout ("Ecstasy"), grandfatherly ("Dry Bread") or grandiloquent ("The Four Winds of the Mind"). "After the Battle" eulogizes his father, who was a high-ranking officer in the army of Napoleon I.

Félix Arvers is tersely characterized in the French encyclopedia *Larousse* as "a poet immortalized by a single poem"—the one translated here. The poet's loved one, so oblivious of him and so "piously true" to her "austere duty"— what is she? A nun? A married woman?

The life of **Gérard de Nerval** was marred by recurrent bouts of madness and ended in suicide. An inveterate traveler (see "Waking Up on a Coach"), he delved deeply into foreign cultures and the teachings of various religions. Only belatedly recognized as a major poet, Nerval's influence on writers of this century has been perhaps more profound than that of any of his fellow Romantics.

Alfred de Musset preceded Frédéric Chopin in the affections of George Sand, the flamboyant female novelist. His poetic style, although basically passionate and Romantic, also has its ironic, intellectual aspects. As is foreshadowed in his poem "Molière," some of his best writing was done in drama.

The controversial poetry of **Charles Baudelaire**, who was virtually a pariah in his own time, has since been widely acclaimed. It has evoked a great deal of scholarly research and many translations. Some of the poems in *Les Fleurs du mal* explore themes and areas of human experience which are not universally accepted as suitable subjects for poetic treatment.

Armand Sully Prudhomme, a philosophical, somewhat melancholy poet, was the first winner (1901) of the Nobel Prize for literature. "The Rendez-vous" is especially noteworthy for its poetic treatment of science.

José-Maria de Heredia was the direct descendant of a Spanish nobleman who figured prominently in Spain's early exploration and colonization of the New World. It is therefore not surprising that many of the sonnets in his collection entitled *Les Trophées*, including the three translated here, deal with historical events and personages.

François Coppée is best known for having written *Le Passant*, a one-act comedy in which the great Sarah Bernhardt played her first starring role. His poetry, with its low-key simplicity of language, reflects his view of himself as "the poet of the common man." In "Paris," for instance, all the places he is fond of in his native city are totally lacking in Parisian glamor.

Maurice Rollinat, unfortunately for his literary reputation, was once dubbed by a critic "a second-rate Baudelaire"—an epithet doubtless suggested by the outlandishness of some of his subject matter. Rollinat was famous for frightening his audiences as he performed his poetry in cabarets such as Le Chat Noir, where he played and sang songs at the piano, sometimes incorporating a model guillotine into his act.

ABOUT THE TRANSLATOR

Born the only son of a school administrator in northwestern Ohio, Kendall Lappin evinced early on a strong affinity for the interplay of languages. After majoring in French and Spanish at DePauw University and achieving fluency in French at Middlebury College, he taught high school language courses (including English) in Fairfield, Illinois until the outbreak of World War II. Upon graduation from the Navy's Japanese Language School in 1944, he served as a junior officer in the Pacific theater. At war's end he was assigned to the U. S. Naval Academy, to teach foreign languages to the midshipmen; soon thereafter he converted to civilian faculty status and made teaching at Annapolis his career, adding (in 1954) a Middlebury M.A. degree in Russian to his qualifications. Since his retirement in 1976 he has been active in literary translation—mostly poetry—from French to English.